PLEASE G

a falcon *littlehawk* book

prayers for children

illustrated by Joyce Badrocke

First published December 1966

Reprinted July 1967, December 1968, January 1970, August 1971

Illustrations and cover Joyce Badrocke, Des.RCA

Overseas agents

EMU Book Agencies Ltd,
511 Kent Street, Sydney, NSW, Australia

CSSM and Crusader Bookroom Society Ltd,
177 Manchester Street, Christchurch, New Zealand

Sunday School Centre Wholesale
Box 3020, Cape Town, South Africa

Published for the Church Pastoral-Aid Society
Falcon Court, 32 Fleet Street, London EC4

Made and printed in Great Britain by
Billing & Sons Limited, Guildford and London

For

ANDREW

and all other children like him

who insist that prayer must be relevant

Contents

Page for grown-ups

This book has a new approach. It is designed to help young children realize that prayer should be a natural part of their exciting everyday lives.

God is interested in everyone and everything, and it is this wonderful fact that we want to reveal to our children.

Small children love looking into pictures, so it is with this thought in mind that Joyce Badrocke has designed her charming illustrations. Every prayer topic has a picture, and it is suggested that parents explore the appropriate picture with their children before they use the suggested prayers.

It will of course be realized that parents should be prepared to adapt slightly any prayers that may not exactly fit the circumstances of a particular child. This is a book for parents and children to share. It is not intended that children should be expected to use it independently, although of course certain older children may prefer to do so.

The 'thinking' and 'thanking' pages at the end of the book are a simple introduction to meditation. We want to make sure that our children do not think that all prayer must be audible. These pages should help them to grasp this fact.

Miss Badrocke and I have enjoyed preparing this book, and we hope that many parents and children will enjoy using it, for if we can learn to enjoy prayer, then indeed we shall need no persuasion to practise it!

BERYL BYE

MARTINS BANK
High Street
New Park
Dear Mr Smith,
We have to inform you
The Cottage
Park Green,
Shipton
July 27th
Dear Bill,
It was lovely
Love
Mum
AUSTIN. FORD. SAAB
BROWNS GARAGE
The Broadway
New Park.
Dear Sir,
Dear Daddy
from Sue

Writing letters

When someone writes a letter, or talks to your Daddy he is called by a special name. It is not always the same name.

YOU would say 'Dear Daddy . . .'
Your grandma would call him
'Dear Bill [*or* Peter *or* Colin] . . .'
The manager at Daddy's bank would write
'Dear Mr Smith . . .'
And the garage man 'Dear Sir . . .'

These are all different ways of speaking or writing to the same person – your Daddy.

We call God by lots of different names but we are always speaking to the same Person.

Sometimes we remember how wonderfully He looks after us and we say 'Heavenly Father'.

Sometimes we think about how well He knows what it is like to live here on earth and we say 'Lord Jesus'.

When we are thinking of how great God is, we call Him 'Almighty God'.

These are all different ways of speaking to the same Person – the one true God.

To Mummy
From Me
x x
2/
so we hope to
see you on next
Sunday. with
love from us all
Rosemary
and Julie
X X
with love to
Granny
from
Stephen x
Happy
Birthday
from
Sue
love
from
Ann

Amen

Do you sometimes add your name to a letter that Mummy has written, or sign neatly on the inside of a birthday card which you are sending to a friend? If you are very small, perhaps you just write a kiss. This is your way of saying that you want the person who is receiving the letter or card to know that it brings your special greeting.

At the end of our prayers to God we usually say 'Amen'. This is our way of saying:

> 'This is my special prayer –
> I want God to know it comes from
> ME!'

BEST
BEST
BEST SEEDS
PEAS
ROTS

HILLTOP FARM

canning factory

FROZEN PEAS

GROCER
JONES

JAM
14 p.

1 Food

Heavenly Father,
Thank You for the warm sunshine and the soft rain that falls upon the farmer's fields so that they will grow corn, and carrots, and swedes, and potatoes, and fresh greens. Thank You for providing enough for our needs so that everyone in our country may be fed with good food. *Amen*

Lord Jesus,
You know that before I wake up in the morning, men and women will be busy in the markets of our towns buying and selling fresh food.

Help those who sell not to be greedy, and those who buy to be fair, so that the food in our shops can be sold at prices that all people can afford. *Amen*

Dear God,
Please bless those who spend their lives working in the factories of our country where food is tinned and frozen to make sure it stays fresh and good to eat.

Help them to be clean and careful in their work, and cheer them up when they become tired of doing the same job over and over again. *Amen*

DRINK A PINTA
REMOVALS
Jones & Son
NORWICH
AMBULANCE
TAXI

STOP

2 Road safety

Dear Heavenly Friend,
Please be with me every time I cross the road or walk along the pavement, so that You can remind me not to rush into the street or cross without looking. Stop me when I forget that it is dangerous to run into the road after a ball, or to take the dog for a walk without a lead, so that I may never be a danger to other people.
Amen

Please God,
Bless the crossing keepers who give up their time to see that boys and girls can cross the road safely. Remind me to thank them every time they take me across the road, so that they know that I am grateful.
Amen

Almighty God,
We pray today for those who drive cars and buses and taxis and big lorries, and especially for Mummy and Daddy as they drive our car. Help them to keep their minds on what they are doing and to know the right thing to do if anything unexpected happens, and help me to sit quietly so that they are not worried by my fidgeting or quarrelling. *Amen*

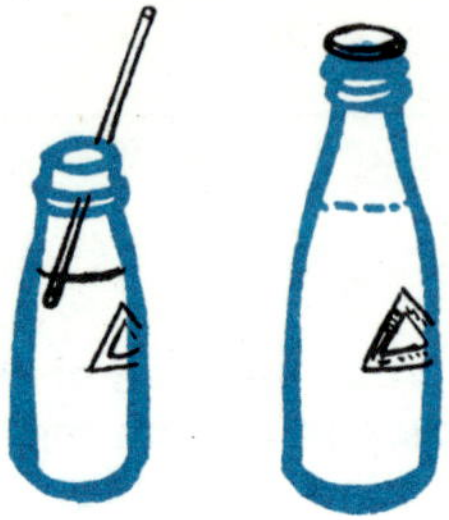

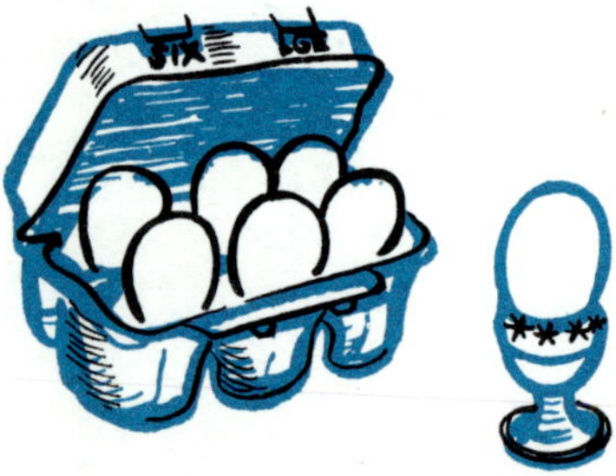
SIX

3 Cows, sheep and chickens

Father God,
Thank You for making cows who give the fresh milk which is so good to drink. Thank You for the nice butter which I spread upon my bread. Thank You for the cream that we enjoy as a special treat. *Amen*

Dear God,
I sometimes forget that the soft wool that is used to make my winter coat and warm jumpers comes from the thick coats of the sheep which You have made. Thank You for looking after me in this way. *Amen*

Lord Jesus,
Nearly every day I have brown or white eggs for my breakfast or my tea. They are so good to eat that I want to thank You for them.

Bless the farmer who looks after the chickens, the men and women who must handle the eggs gently as they pack them into boxes, and the shopkeeper who sells them to my Mummy. *Amen*

BAKER
HIGH CLASS JEWELLERS
TICK &

I've lost my Mummy!...

4 Policemen and judges, and people who do wrong

Dear God,
Please look after the policemen and policewomen of our land whose job it is to see that people behave in an honest and lawful way. Be with them in the night, when they walk the streets alone to make sure of our safety. Give them the right words to say when they must bring sad news; and when they must face danger or difficulty help them to be brave. *Amen*

Lord Jesus Christ,
We pray for the men and women, and boys and girls, who will today be tempted to cheat or steal, or to do some other very wrong thing. Help them to be strong and to turn away from bad thoughts and deeds, and to turn to You who can always help them to be good. *Amen*

Gracious Lord,
We ask You to guide the men and women who are judges and magistrates in the courts of our land. Teach them how to be wise and fair, so that those who come before them may be judged fairly and punished rightly, and so learn to lead better lives. *Amen*

5 Holidays

Loving Heavenly Father,

We thank You for the joy of holidays and all the fun we have in them.

Thank You for sunny and windy days, and the feel of the warm, fresh rain on our faces. Thank You for fathers to play with us, for mothers to cook and care for us, and for brothers and sisters and friends to share all these things with us. *Amen*

Dear Lord Jesus,

Thank You for making the great sea and the big and little creatures that live in it.

Thank You for the pretty shells and the tiny fish that swim in the rock pools.

Thank You for the sand, and the way the sea goes in and out.

Thank You for the salty taste of the spray upon our lips.

Thank You for putting us in the world so that we can enjoy these lovely things. *Amen*

Wonderful God,

We praise You for the beauty of the countryside. For big trees and small flowers. For tiny streams and great rushing rivers and waterfalls. For hills where we can race and play. For valleys where we are sheltered from the wind. For moors with their carpet of pink heather and for forests where we can be quiet and hear the sounds of growing and living things.

Amen

6 Astronauts

Almighty God,
We ask for Your special blessing upon the astronauts of every country whose love of adventure makes them want to explore the space beyond our earth.

Help them to be brave in danger, calm in difficulty, and peaceful during the long time that they must spend alone. *Amen*

Dear Lord,
We pray for the wives and children who are left behind to wait and watch and wonder, while husbands and fathers are away on lonely and dangerous jobs. Comfort them, we ask You, and bring those they love safely home again. *Amen*

Great God,
Who has made all things wise and wonderful. We ask You to give clever brains and careful hands to the ones who plan and make the wonderful machines that carry men on journeys of discovery. Let no lack of thought or careless act cause harm to those who fly in these space craft. *Amen*

O God our Maker and Creator,
Thank You for giving us the excitement of sharing in man's landings on the moon. Grant that the moon-shots may assist man to realize more of Your greatness, and help him to use the information he gains to make the universe a happier place. *Amen*

7 Healthy bodies and happy games

Dear Lord,
We thank You for giving us strong and healthy bodies so that we can run and skip and dance and play. Remind us to use our young hands and arms to carry things for those older and weaker than ourselves, and our sturdy legs to run errands for those who cannot move as quickly as we can. *Amen*

Almighty God,
Who in Your great wisdom made the world and put the sun to shine above it. We praise You for the sweetness of the air, and the warmth of the sun, that helps us and all living things to grow. *Amen*

Lord Jesus,
Please help us to be cheerful when we lose a game as well as happy when we win it.

Teach us to share with others their disappointments and be pleased when they do well. *Amen*

8 Summer and winter

Dear God,
I want to thank You for all the special joys that the long summer days bring.

For the hot days when we can eat our meals out of doors.

For the fun of splashing in our paddling pool in the garden.

For new potatoes with their papery skins and the pop of the green pea pods as I shell them for Mummy.

For strawberries and raspberries and ice cream, and cold lemon and orange squash to drink when I am thirsty.

Thank You for all these lovely things, dear God.
Amen

Father in Heaven,
Thank You for giving us so many different kinds of weather so that we can enjoy so many different things.

Thank You for crisp frosty days when our breath turns into fog if we huff into the air.

Thank You for the snow and the happy games we have with snowmen and snowballs and sledges.

Thank You for cosy beds and cuddly hot water bottles and the happy feeling that we are loved and cared for. *Amen*

9 My family

Dear Lord Jesus,
Thank You for giving me to a Mummy and Daddy who love me so much. Show me how I can help them both in small ways. Remind me to get Daddy's slippers when he is tired, and to lay the table for Mummy when she is busy, and help me to do what they say without arguing. *Amen*

Dear Jesus,
We are so happy to have a little baby living in our house. Show me how to look after him and help me always to be gentle, and kind and loving, and not to shout or make other loud noises that might frighten him. *Amen*

Dear God,
I am so glad I have a Granny and Grandad to visit and to come and stay with us. Help me not to be cross if they sometimes do not hear what I say, and to be willing to post letters or run to the shops for them, whenever they ask me. *Amen*

10 Fishermen and sailors

Dear God,
Please bless the fishermen who work while I am asleep so that I can have fresh fish to eat. Help them to be cheerful and good tempered as they go out in the wind and rain, and help me to be thankful as I eat the nice fish that they have caught. *Amen*

Dear Lord,
Keep in safety those who sail great ships across the sea to other countries. Give the Captain wisdom. Help the crew to be obedient and watchful. Give trust and understanding to the passengers, and bring all of them safely to their journey's end. *Amen*

Almighty God,
We praise You for the wonderful sea which You have made.

We praise You for the little waves dancing in the sunlight; for the crash of the big waves upon the shore; for the silver pathway of the moon's light shining across calm water; for all those who love the sea and spend their lives working near it and on it. For all this we praise and thank You. *Amen*

11 Clothes

Dear God,
You have given the birds feathers, and cows and dogs hairy coats, and I have nice clothes to keep me warm and dry.

Thank You for giving me a Daddy who will work hard and earn money so that I can go with Mummy to the shops to buy them. *Amen*

Heavenly Father,
When the rain comes tumbling down and makes splashy puddles on the path I like to put on my wellingtons and jump in them.

I want to thank You for giving me my mackintosh and waterproof hat and rubber boots so that I can go out and enjoy the rainy days without getting wet. *Amen*

Lord Jesus,
You know how much I like wearing my best clothes when I go to church or to a party, or out to tea.

Thank You for my special clothes which help me to look smart and neat, and Lord Jesus, please make me as nice inside, as I look outside, when I am wearing them. *Amen*

EIIR
DRINKA PINTA
FARM DAIRY
BUNN'S
BAKERY

12 The milkman, the baker, and the postman

Dear God,
You know we sometimes take for granted the milkman who puts the bottles of milk on our doorsteps every single day. We forget he must get up very early, while we are still asleep, and do his job in rain, and snow, and wind and cold. Remind us to say 'thank you' to him when he calls, and to be understanding if he leaves us the wrong number of bottles. *Amen*

Lord Jesus,
Please bless the men and women who work in hot steamy kitchens mixing and baking the nice new loaves which the baker brings to our door. When they are tired and bored with their job, help them to remember that it is an important one, and help me to be grateful and not waste any of the bread which has been made and brought to me. *Amen*

Father God,
I like the postman calling at my house with letters and postcards from my friends. May I be willing and cheerful about writing letters or drawing pictures, so that I can bring happiness to those people who receive them. *Amen*

13 Our church

Heavenly Father,
We thank You that we are able to worship in Your House on Your day. We pray for all those people in other lands who must worship secretly or in fear of punishment. Make them brave, and help them to be made stronger by our prayers. *Amen*

Dear Father God,
Please bless our minister and all his helpers as they work for You in this place.

When they are tired refresh them.

When they are sad cheer them.

When they have too much to do, show us how we can help them.

In Your Name we ask it. *Amen*

Dear Lord Jesus,
You gave Your life for us, and yet there seems to be so little that we can give to You. Please accept the money that we give for Your work in this and other lands, and help us to give because we want to, and not because we ought, for we know that You like us to give in a cheerful way. *Amen*

Dear Lord,
Please help us to make our Church a friendly place where people will feel that because we love and care about You, we love and care about them as well. Help us to smile back when people smile at us, and to say 'Hullo' even if we feel shy inside. *Amen*

S M T W T F S
· 1 2 3 4 5 6
7 8 9 10 11 12 13
14 15 16 17 18 19 20
21 22 23 24 25 26 27
30 31 · · ·
happy Birthday!
Best Wishes
Ann

14 Birthdays

Dear Lord Jesus,
You know that today is my birthday. Thank You for bringing me safely through another year. Thank You for making me taller so that I can reach light switches and door handles, and for making me stronger so that I can jump higher and carry heavier things.

Thank You for making me more clever so that I can understand harder words, and read and write and draw much more easily. Help me to grow each year in every way and specially help me to grow more like You. *Amen*

Heavenly Father,
I want to thank You for all the presents and cards I have received today. It is lovely to have so many people who care for me enough to take trouble to remember that it is my birthday. Please bless every person who has been kind to me today and help me to share all my new books and toys with my friends so that they can enjoy my birthday as well. *Amen*

Dear God,
Please bless my Mummy and Daddy who have given me such a happy day. I have enjoyed everything so much. Thank You for giving me a Mummy to make me a birthday cake and a Daddy who can mend toys if they break or go wrong.

I know there are lots of boys and girls who do not have a special fuss made when it is their birthday. Show me if there is anyone like that in my road or school so that I can be specially nice to them. *Amen*

yesterday
was wet
to-day is
sunny
to-day is
monday
To-day
Ann
will give
out the
Books
we are going to the
shops: we are going to
buy
Flowers
The Farm
ABC
WONDER
BOOK
ABC
JGW

15 Those who teach and those who learn

Dear Lord Jesus,
You spent so much of Your time on earth teaching people, that we know You understand the needs of all those who have to teach others. We ask for Your special blessing today upon our teachers, both at Day School and Sunday School. Help them as they read and think so that they may be able to teach, and give them patience when children in their classes do not want, or try, to learn. *Amen*

Father of all men,
We pray today for boys and girls of other lands who go to our schools. Give them courage as they live and work with those whose words and ways are so different from their own, and help us to be especially loving and friendly to them. *Amen*

O Lord,
You know that sometimes we do not like going to school and learning our lessons. Help us to remember that You want us to work well so that when we are grown up we shall be able to do interesting jobs that will please You, and help others. *Amen*

BEA
BEA
BEA
HW
MC

16 Travel by land, sea, and air

Almighty God,
Thank You for making men clever enough to invent railway engines and motor cars, and for making men careful enough to drive them so that we can go quickly and safely from place to place.

Thank You for the fun we have travelling in them when we go to exciting places or visit our friends.
Amen

Lord Jesus,
We know that the sea is deep and can be very dangerous. We know that Your special friends were sometimes frightened in boats even though You were there.

Be with all those who travel upon the sea, whether in great liners or little fishing boats. Be with all those who travel under the sea in submarines.

Guard them from danger and help them in difficulty and give your special protection to the brave men in lifeboats who risk their lives to go out and help ships in distress. *Amen*

Lord God,
We pray for those who pilot aeroplanes and the mechanics who look after and mend them.

We pray for the stewards and stewardesses who see that passengers are comfortable.

Help them to keep their minds upon their work and to be wise about taking rest. Help them to be patient with people who make them feel cross and to do every little job carefully so that all those who travel by air may do so in safety. *Amen*

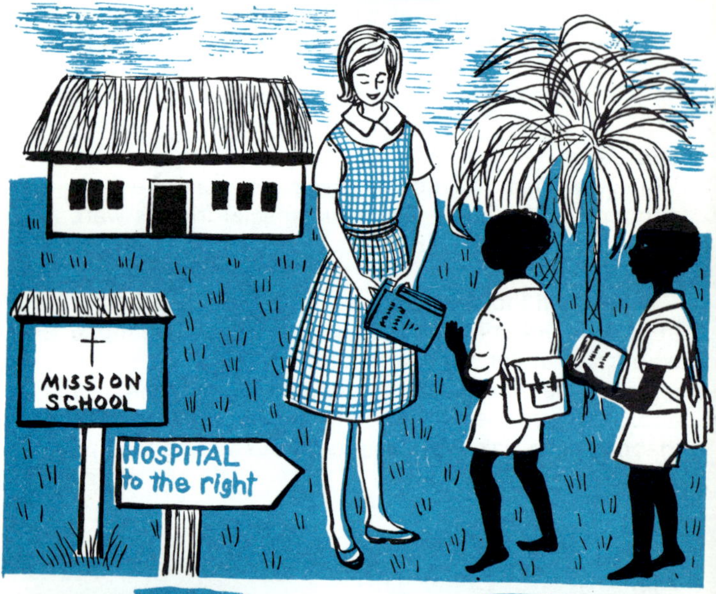
MISSION SCHOOL
HOSPITAL to the right

St LUKE

MAF

17 Missionaries

Dear Lord,
We know that before You went back to Heaven you told your special friends that You wanted the good news about Yourself to be told to everyone in the world. Please bless the men and women who are doing as You asked them, and have left their homes and families to live in other countries, and among different people, so that they can teach them about You.

Help them as they go back to school to learn to speak and write the language of foreign people and cheer them up when they feel sad or homesick. *Amen*

Almighty God,
Please bless the men who pilot the little aeroplanes that are used to carry missionaries and Bibles and books to people who cannot easily be reached in any other way.

Help them to know that You are with them and keep them in safety we pray You. *Amen*

Dear Father God,
Thank You for giving us Your special Book and help us to understand when the words seem rather hard. Please bless the men and women who are working to change the Bible into other languages. Please guide them so that one day everyone, everywhere, will be able to read the Bible in their own language and know the story of Your love and care for us. *Amen*

HOSPITAL
casualties to the right
AMBULANCE
ST JOHN
staff parking only
DOSE

18 Doctors and all those who work in hospitals

Dear Father God,
I pray today . . .

For the doctors who have learned to make sick people better and to take away pain.

For the nurses and ambulance men whose arms and feet often ache because they spend so many hours of the day and night hurrying from bed to bed and looking after people who cannot look after themselves.

For the specially trained men and women who show such patience in teaching damaged legs to walk again and helping hurt muscles to work again.

For the cleaners and cooks in hospitals who cheerfully work at the ordinary and uninteresting jobs so that the buildings are warm and clean and comfortable and the sick people have the right kind of food to make them well and strong again.

For all these people we pray and ask Your Blessing.
Amen

MY JESUS BOOK
Mary Anne

19 Lonely people

Dear Lord,
We are so used to having lots of people around us, that we sometimes forget to pray for people who must live their lives in lonely places. Please bless the light-house keepers who watch the dangerous and rocky parts of our coasts, so that ships can come and go in safety. When it is rough and stormy outside, help them to be calm and peaceful inside themselves, and may they sometimes use the times they are alone to think about You. *Amen*

Lord Jesus Christ,
We are thinking today about the men in the weather ships whose job it is to note every change of rain, and clouds, and wind and storm, so that people can fly and sail safely around the world. Help them to watch carefully, and speak clearly, and write plainly, so that lives may be saved because of their care. *Amen*

Dear Jesus,
Please bless the old and ill people who live by themselves in a tiny room, and can seldom enjoy the fun and beauty of the busy and jolly world in which we live. Help us to think about any lonely people who live near us, and put into our minds some good ideas about how we can cheer them up. *Amen*

UNICEF
United Nations
Children's Fund

Aid for
children

Helping
refugees

W.H.O.
world health
organisation

World Food
programme

UNESCO
Education &
culture

International
co-operation

Working
for peace

Sharing
skills

20 The United Nations Organization

Holy Spirit of God,
Please guide the leaders of many different countries at the meetings where they try, by working together, to make the world a better and a safer place.

Help them to want peace rather than power, and show them how they can share the food in the world so that no one need be hungry. *Amen*

Dear Lord Jesus,
We know that there are many people in the world who do not know how to read and write, and have never been taught how to make their land grow enough food to eat. Choose the right men and women to go and teach these people so that they may learn how to help themselves. *Amen*

Dear God,
At the times when homes are swept away by great storms, and food crops are lost through heavy rains or terribly strong winds, show the leaders of countries how they can give the most help. May those who have plenty give to those who have little or nothing, and show me and my family if there is any way we can do something useful by giving money, or warm clothes, or blankets, to feed and warm cold, and homeless, and hungry people. *Amen*

EIIR
THE DAILY NEWS
QUEEN AND PRINCE TO
SIT NEW
AND IN
NEW YEAR
PRIME MINISTER SAYS WE ARE
2½P
NEW PENCE
10

21 The Royal Family

Almighty God,
Lord of all, and King of Kings, Please bless our Queen as she seeks to serve You in the very special place in which You have put her.

Help her to be wise in all her thoughts and ways, and give her patience and understanding as she meets and talks with so many different people every day. *Amen*

Dear God,
We thank You for Prince Philip, who is able to share with our Queen in her many duties.

We thank You because he is not afraid to speak up for things that are right, and to speak strongly against things that he believes to be wrong. Lead and guide him in all he says and does we pray You. *Amen*

Dear Father God,
We ask Your blessing on the children of our Queen. We know there must be times when they want very much to be with their parents who are so often called away from them. Help them to be brave when they must say good-bye in front of other people, and give them special joy and happiness at the times they are able to be together, *Amen*

Lord God Almighty,
Please bless Charles, Prince of Wales, and his sister Princess Anne as they travel on visits of goodwill, both in our own land and to countries across the seas. Keep them in safety as they journey, give them enjoyment of their work, and may their warmth and friendliness help to bring closer together people of different nations and customs throughout the world. *Amen*

merry
Christmas
To
From

22 Christmas

Dear Lord Jesus,
I know that today is Your birthday, and birthdays are a time for giving gifts. I would like to give You a present, dear Lord, but I know the only one You really want is the gift of myself. I want to belong to You, and I want You to use me so that I know that I am yours.

Tell me when You want me to be helpful, kind or obedient, by speaking inside me with a voice that only I can hear. And when I forget, please remind me that I am my birthday gift to You and belong to You. *Amen*

Lord Jesus Christ,
You were too little to understand about the presents that the wise men brought to You, but I am big enough to enjoy my presents and to know that people have spent their money in buying them and their time to wrap them up. Help me to remember to thank every person who has given me a gift and to treat my presents carefully and to share them too. *Amen*

Dear God,
I thank You . . .

For the bright cards that the postman brings to remind us about Your birthday.

For the little cribs that remind us what Christmas is about.

For the carols with their jolly tunes we love to sing.

For the bulgy stocking by our bed on Christmas morning.

For our church where we go to say thank You for all these happy things. *Amen*

happy Easter
HAPPY EASTER

23 Easter

Dear Lord Jesus,
Today is such a happy day because we remember the time when You came back to life again after cruel men had caused your death. We know how happy Your special friends were when they saw You again, and we are happy too – because now we know that no one who loves You need be afraid to die, because dying only means going into a special kind of sleep and waking up with You in Heaven. *Amen*

Dear Father,
I have had an Easter egg given to me today.

It makes me think of new lives because I know that sometimes real eggs turn into clean little fluffy lively chicken, who begin a new life once they are outside their egg shell.

I know I can have a clean new life if I ask You to forgive me all the wrong things I have done and help me to be good.

Please forgive me and help me on this Easter day. *Amen*

Lord Jesus,
We are so glad to know that you are alive today, looking after us and watching over us at school, at home, and while we play. Please help us to be good and to know what is right and what is wrong. *Amen*

cheat!...
ow!....
miow.....
me first!
Go and help Sue
to put her toys
away....
Shan't!
It's not
fair!....
I didn't
do it!....
Be unkind!....
Is
anyone
looking?
Sweets

A 'thinking' page

We do not always need to use words if we want to pray to God – 'Thinking' prayers can go on inside our heads without any 'speaking' words at all.

The pictures on the other page are to help you make up a 'thinking' prayer to God inside your own head.

Look at them carefully and see if you have done any of the wrong things today that the children in the pictures are doing. Or perhaps you have done different wrong things that are not actually pictured?

Think about the wrong things you have done, and then close your eyes and say 'sorry' to God. And have you remembered to say sorry to Mummy and Daddy as well?

HAPPY
BIRTHDAY!
5

HOLY
BIBLE

GIANT
PUZZLE
S
O

STORIES

A 'thanking' page

Does Mummy or Daddy have to remind you to say 'Thank you' when someone gives you something?

Sometimes we need reminding to say 'Thank you' to God for all the good things He gives to us, and the pictures on the other page will help you too.

Which of the pictured things do you enjoy most?

Choose some of them and then whisper 'Thank you, God' so that your prayer is known only to God and you.

THE END

The Hill of the Dead

is the first in the authentic and violent series of the savage days of the Roman Empire – *The Eagles*.

The Hill of the Dead

Andrew Quiller

Mayflower

Granada Publishing Limited
First published in 1976 by Mayflower Books Ltd
Frogmore, St Albans, Herts AL2 2NF

A Mayflower Original

Made and printed in Great Britain by
Cox & Wyman Ltd
London, Reading and Fakenham
Set in Intertype Plantin

This is for Nick Austin – an editor who is both nice *and* believes in the importance of integrity. That makes him rather rare and I'm glad to think he's a friend. I refer him to the words of Martial:

Non est, crede mihi, sapientis dicere: 'Vivam':
Sera nimis vita est crastina: vive hodie.

ONE

High over the Colosseum, a tiny speck in the clear blue of the summer sky, a hawk hung motionless and stared blankly down at the yellow sand of the arena. Watching the figures of men as they darted and ran, wondering why some fell and lay so still. The red of the blood as it seeped into the sand spoke of death. And death meant meat. But the bird had lived long enough around Rome to know that the meat that appeared far below it would soon vanish.

Incuriously, it tipped a wing and swooped away on a current of warm air, diving towards the woods that lay a few miles to the north, and where it knew there would be rabbits. Behind it, in the arena, the slaughter continued.

In the highest tiers of the maenianum, those reserved for ladies, Poppaea sat back in her seat, fanning at her forehead with a languid hand. Although her nails were bitten down almost to the pale moons, they were still undoubtedly the hands of a lady, and she smiled vaguely to herself at that thought. No great red calluses across the palms like a servant-girl. Her husband, Helvius Geminus, would have thrown one of his temper fits if he'd ever seen her doing anything with those hands. Except a little embroidery, perhaps. Though that bored her.

Poppaea munched another date, spitting out the stone on the warm stones near her feet. Idly, she glanced around her, waving a greeting to a couple of her friends who had just taken seats a little higher up. They'd obviously had their lunch and then come along to watch the big combat. Next on the programme, so one of the attendants had told her. The thought made her go weak at the knees, and she pressed her thighs hard together, feeling a delicious dampness.

The sand had been raked clean once more and the last of the filling performances was about to start. The break at midday was always for the slaughter of convicted criminals, in as ingenious a way as the promoter could think up.

Another date went the same way as the others had done.

A burst of cheering from the packed ranks of the slaves, stacked higher up, their dark-clothed rows seeming to climb up into the sun. Poppaea turned back from her scrutiny of who was sitting with whom among her acquaintances and concentrated her attention on the arena again. The great striped velarium, hung to give some shade to the better-off spectators, flapped suddenly in a breeze coming in from the sea, its surface rippling like a pool of sullen water.

At either end of the great arena stood braziers, pillars of heat wavering up from their glowing charcoal. By them stood a couple of slaves – massive black men, armed with iron-tipped whips. Poppaea gazed at them for a moment, wondering absently if her husband, Marcus, might not be persuaded that a black would decorate their new summer villa on the Bay of Naples. His work as a cloth merchant often kept him in the city, and his loving wife was alone with her slaves for days on end. A black, if he was as well-endowed as these fellows seemed to be, could be a very pleasant distraction.

To the blare of trumpets, coming from the direction of the editor's box, the two men who were about to die marched slowly out. Or, she noticed with a shiver of pleasure, they were led out. Both were young men, clad only in a short tunic of stained wool. And both had been blinded. Not with an iron, as had been her first hope, but by having strips of cloth wound tightly around their heads. To the amusement of the crowd, swelling at every moment as the time grew nearer for Vulpus to make his appearance, the shorter of the men tripped over his own feet and was only held upright by the slave who led him along.

'He's had it already!!' shouted out a fat slave directly behind Poppaea.

'Come on the cripple!! Give him a crutch so he can stand up!' bellowed another.

'If he can't walk, I bet the skinny bastard won't be able to fight either!' roared a third man.

Both men were given swords, and they were placed a few paces from each other. The master of ceremonies in the arena itself looked up at the editor in his box, shaded and cool, waiting for him to turn his attention from the young woman alongside him. Finally, with an idle wave of the hand, the man gave the signal for the fight to begin.

Though it was hardly a fight.

The blacks at either end loped forward, their feet hissing in the hot sand, the whips trailing behind them like drugged snakes. It would be for them to make sure that the two men, both condemned for attacking a soldier two nights before and slitting his throat for a purse of silver, didn't back away. If the bite of their whips proved an insufficient incentive, then there were always the hot irons, shimmering in the metal braziers at opposite ends of the arena.

Bewildered by the sudden silence, the two men stood quite still, one feebly waving his sword at the air in front of him.

Throughout the morning there had been the animals, fighting against each other and against men. It had been poor stuff, with dusty spavined beasts and men whose sole concern seemed to be staying alive, rather than entertaining the crowd. There had been hissing from the slaves. Hissing that had spread to the lower seats. The editor in his box could be seen becoming more and more angry, finally sending in blacks with whips to speed up the action.

Poppaea smiled at the memory of what had been the best moment of the morning. A lioness had managed to catch one of the men, and clasped him to her with her forepaws, while he struggled to get free, turning his face away from the rank breath and the yellow teeth. But it hadn't been the teeth that she'd used. As they'd rolled together in the bloody sand, the beast had brought up her powerful back legs, and raked at his stomach, the claws tearing his flesh apart in a red ruin.

His intestines had dropped out from the slit in his body, trailing in the dust like the greasy fronds of some exotic plant. The lioness had been distracted for a moment by the scream of another man, and had dropped her victim, padding away across the arena. The wretch had staggered to his feet and tried to run away, but he kept tripping over his own tripes, dangling and snagging at his bare feet.

Finally he took the shouted advice of the crowd and bent down and scooped up his intestines, draping them over his arm like a senator with a new toga. With his other hand he tried to hold the lips of the gaping wound together, but the blood still poured from him.

He had been a savage from . . . Poppaea could never remember the barbaric names of all the enemies of Rome, and he had tried to call for mercy in his gobbling tongue, which had amused the crowd all the more. There was such an uproar that hardly anyone even bothered to turn their thumbs downwards in the sign for death. In his box the editor who was giving the games was suddenly restored to his good humour by the change in the mob's spirits, and leaned out over the balcony of his box so that he might see better.

The rest of the men were quickly slain, and the beasts with no corpse to mangle were suddenly aware of the one man still on his feet and had begun to close in. But the barbarian wasn't even aware of them, and continued to call and gesture to the crowd. His shredded stomach didn't seem to bother him at all, apart from a gesture of irritation when a strand of it slipped from his arm and stuck to his bloodied thighs. He had flicked it away with the same kind of motion a man might make if a fly had bothered him during a meal, and the crowd had loved him for it.

Two of the young equites had jumped to their feet in their front row and begun to try and rouse a chant for freedom for the man, though all the regulars knew well enough that nobody ever came through with that sort of wound. What was some kind of miracle was that he still stood, with the sand about his feet turned almost to red mud with the outpouring of his bright blood.

Poppaea shuffled her legs, remembering how she'd laughed so much that she thought for a moment that she'd lost control of her bladder. It was well enough that the stinking slaves did what they had to where they stood in the upper rows, but it was not the done thing for a lady.

The crowd had begun to take up the chant, and it was more than possible that the editor would have signalled for mercy, but the beasts got there first. The cheering and shouting faded away like the dew on the roofs of a summer morning. Oblivious to his death stalking up behind him, the savage carried on with his tirade, waving his arms around, seeming to forget his appalling wound.

It was a bear that reached him first. A great shaggy black monster, hauling itself up on its hind legs, so that it stood only a hand shorter than the man. One sandy paw reached out and touched him on the shoulder, like the familiar greeting of a friend. The silence erupted again into shrieks of laughter as the barbarian, without even looking round, pushed the animal away from him, like a rich merchant dismissing a testy creditor.

And then the joke was over.

Swift as a bolt of lightning from Olympus, the bear struck at him. Its paw smashed into the side of his head, knocking him flying across the arena, blood spraying from the new wound in his skull. Yet he still made a last attempt to rise to his feet, struggling up on his hands and knees. The bear dropped to all fours and lumbered clumsily after him, snarling at a lion that showed signs of getting in its way.

With the casual ease of a schoolmaster cuffing a naughty boy, the animal flicked out a paw, hitting the barbarian under the chin. There was the clear snap of breaking bone, and his head flopped backwards on his shoulders, the sightless eyes staring up at the gold disc of the sun.

When the animals were in the games, there was rarely much chance of saving the corpses. Since the beasts were kept hungry to make them more vicious, it would have meant slaughtering them all. And a few draggled corpses were never worth the expense of valuable animals. So Charon remained out of sight, and the doors of the Porta Libitinaria, the Gate of Death, remained firmly closed.

From the thoughts of past killing, Poppaea wrenched her mind back to the present combat, though she knew well enough it would not give one hundredth of the thrills of seeing Vulpus in action.

The two convicted criminals were still feeling their way towards each other, while the crowd bayed for more action. At the beginning of the break, less than an hour ago, there had been sixteen of them, but they had each fought before. Eight pairs. Then the winners in four pairs. The winners of that in two pairs, though one of the previous winners had died of his wounds, giving a free passage to the taller of the two who now faced each other in the final fight.

And the winner?

Tomorrow there were more games and he would start all over again. Skill didn't really come into it, and the winner of the previous day never won through two days running. If he had done, then he'd simply have died on the third day. All of them were doomed to die.

Which always meant that the men were never that enthusiastic to exchange blows. In turn, that was why the blacks urged them on, cracking the lashes across their naked backs, until the blood spurted from the weals and they moved forward, trying to listen above the noise of the mob for the sound of the other's feet.

It was the taller man who got the first blow in. A high, slicing cut, biting in under his opponent's ribs, sending him staggering back, sword flailing at the air. Poppaea cried out for the first blooding along with hundreds of others, feeling a tremor of excitement shiver through her loins as it always did at the sight of blood.

The wounded man tried to cry out, but his tongue had been ripped from his mouth before the contests even began, and all that came out was a low gobbling, like an angry fowl.

'Lay us an egg!' bellowed out a voice that Poppaea recognized as belonging to one of her own slaves. Sextus, the kitchen slave with only one eye. She carefully avoided turning round in case he saw her there and gossiped to the rest of her servants. For a lady to go alone would not please her husband, and she knew from previous unhappy experiences how the tongues of slaves could clack.

But now the battle was finally joined. The Nubians withdrew out of range of the flailing weapons, knowing from their own experience that they were not likely to be needed again, and also aware that these doomed men were likely to cut at anything that they heard or sensed moving.

The end came in a flurry of blows almost too quick for the eye to follow. Tall man cut short man on the inside of the thigh, narrowly missing the big artery that would have ended the fight there and then. But it made short man step back, his hands falling to his sides, his sword temporarily forgotten as he groped for a wound he could feel but not see.

His opponent stepped in after him, his short sword hissing in an arc of death, aiming at his throat. But he was fighting a shorter man, and his blow sliced neatly through the bandage that was wound about his enemy's head. The gasp ran clean round the baking Colosseum as the strips of dirty linen dropped from his head like the rotting bandages from an Egyptian mummy. Despite the deep wound in his leg, the smaller man suddenly had the most overwhelming advantage possible.

He could now see, while his opponent still groped his way towards him, stone-blind.

The blacks both looked round for orders, confused by the swift change of events. Uncertain whether or not to stop the fight. The mob had instantly divided into those who wanted to see the shorter man win, and had wagered on him doing precisely that. And those who thought that the tall man should also have his blindfold removed to make the combat more equal.

But the short man wasn't about to stand there and let anyone decide his fate for him. Tugging the bandages away from his head, so that they drooped around his shoulders and flapped at his feet, he took one sideways step, and then lunged at his opponent.

It was a perfect killing blow. Upwards, under the ribs, bursting the heart and tearing the lungs into ribbons. Without a sound the tall man threw up his arms and collapsed backwards on the hot sand. Blood flowed in a scarlet river from his chest, soaking into the arena floor. Before either of the blacks could make a move to defend themselves, the doomed criminal hacked them both down. One with an arm sliced off at the shoulder and the other clutching his groin.

The crowd cheered this spirited defence and it even seemed for a moment that the man might live. But the wound that he had received had weakened him. The editor had waved a hand to the assistants below him, and they had come running in, ready to kill or disarm the man, at the whim of their master. The short man, streaming blood over his legs, turned to run away from them, his little legs twinkling across the sand. Which turned the crowd's cheers to laughter, and ribald laughter as his loincloth dropped off, revealing his pale buttocks and dangling genitals. Poppaea stared with interest at this point, but the poor wretch was sadly endowed and of no concern to her.

One of the women slaves – a strapping woman with dyed hair – called out: 'Throw that one back! He's too little for me!!'

There was some confusion as nobody knew what the editor wanted. Some of the men in the arena were already hefting their javelins, while others simply ran after the wounded man, trying to head him off from the gates.

With the abruptness of a summer storm, the decision was taken. Head rolling with exhaustion, the short figure staggered on, then tried to look back over his shoulder at his pursuers. And tripped over his own feet.

He dropped forwards on to the sand, one arm flung out in front of him, like a runner desperately trying to break the line and win. His other arm was crumpled awkwardly under him.

The arm holding the short sword.

The point of the sword smashed between his upper ribs, bursting out between his shoulder-blades in a welter of blood. For a moment the body kicked and thrashed, the legs seeming as though they were trying to carry on running. Then it jerked upwards and lay still.

The crowd applauded the fine ending while the editor smiled at a satisfactory conclusion to what hadn't been the best day's games he'd ever put on. Even when things had been going badly the young man had still found consolation in the knowledge that he had Vulpus up his sleeve. Vulpus wasn't just good; he was the very best. That was why so much money had changed hands to obtain him. The gladiator fought only on special occasions, and it was said that Vulpus in the arena meant a thousand votes for the man giving the show.

While the blood still pumped like a miniature fountain from the back of the silent corpse, the mob turned to the more serious business of the day. Eating and drinking, and getting their wagers on the next combat. With Vulpus it was hard to find anyone fool enough to take a bet against him at any odds. It was more a question of betting on how and when he would make the kill.

Poppaea slipped another date into her round little mouth, chewing at it, feeling a pang of discomfort from a cavity in one of her upper teeth. It crossed her mind that she would have to go and have it drawn, but the thought of the butchers with their pincers and metal hammers made her wince. To take her mind off that unpleasant thought, she watched the bodies being removed and the sand cleaned and raked.

A group of slaves came running lightly into the arena far below her. First came the figure of Hermes, carrying the rod of twined serpents, heated in one of the braziers so that it glowed dull red. Going quickly from body to body the slim man bent over them and applied the heated tip of the caduceus to their flesh, making sure that life had indeed fled. Smoke drifted up from the scorched corpses, carried by the light wind. Poppaea was glad to see it drift away from her, for the odour of burned meat always made her feel a little ill.

Behind Hermes came the frightening figure of Charon. His face hidden under a great bird-like mask, a cloak about his shoulders. Childhood fears came fluttering back to the watching matron, and she pattered a prayer to the shade of her father to keep her from the spirits of the night.

Charon carried a small hammer which he struck against the temple of each body, claiming it for his own. That ritual done, a horse was led in, dragging ropes behind it. At the end of the ropes were metal hooks. Slaves casually pushed them through the back of the ankles of the corpses, so that they gripped between the tendon and the bone, and they were then dragged out of the Colosseum, leaving a twin furrow of blood in the sand, to vanish through the gate of Libitina, goddess of funerary rites.

It was nearly time. Poppaea sucked at her teeth, breathing in the cooler air, springing from the perfumed water now being sprayed by the slaves. There was the creaking of ropes as the pulleys caught up the slack on the massive shade, moving it a little to allow for the movement of the sun in the cloudless heavens.

The last slave scampered from the arena, having turned over the bloody sand and sprinkled water to lay the choking dust. The vast area below the tiers of spectators looked as clean and virginal as it had at the beginning of the morning. The stage was set and awaited the entry of its main actors for the performance of the day.

As the trumpets brayed out, and the orchestra began to play the entrance music, Poppaea shuffled forwards on her hard seat, feeling the lacework of her leather underclothes sticking to her flesh with the heat and the excitement. Vaguely she noticed that the bottom of her gown was stained with dust, and the stitching of the purple hem, proclaiming her to be a woman of virtue, had come unpicked. When she returned home later, there would be time to give her personal maidservant a good thrashing for that, but there were more important things to do.

Surreptitiously, almost without her seeming aware of it, Poppaea's hand, with its chewed finger-nails, crept up under her white gown, and she began to touch herself on the secret places of her body, wet with excitement. Her mouth opened and she sucked in the hot air through parted lips. She was nearly ready.

Far below her, in one of the maze of passages that ran beneath the Colosseum, two old men, both over forty years of age, stood together near one of the corridors leading to the arena. Knowing that the gladiators would pass near them and they would be able to touch them for luck. It was cool down there, among the traders and the whores, parading their soiled wares, some of the women wearing men's togas to proclaim their calling. As if there could be any doubt of it.

The men were old friends. Both luckier than nearly all of their contemporaries. Born way back at the time of the clumsy, stammering Claudius, they had lived through the rule of six Emperors. Nero, Galba, Otho, Vitellius, Vespasian – who'd begun the Colosseum, and Titus, who'd finished it. Now the few coins that jingled in their purses bore the head of another. Domitian.

Decius and Paulus were both gladiators of some fame and honour in their day, and both had been lucky enough to win the rudis, the wooden staff of freedom, *and* both had been given the papers of emancipation making them free men. Their master, a rich politician, had freed them in a magnanimous gesture many years back. And now they still came to the games and helped out as stewards, showing the people to their seats. Occasionally risking a few denarii on a fancy.

'Soon be here,' muttered Paulus, peering out along the corridor towards the white blaze of the arena.

'What?'

'I said they'll soon be here,' he said, raising his voice against the swelling music and the cheering from the mob above them. Down below it was quieter, as most of the pedlars had packed up and gone to watch with the others. The whores had left their parading and strutting, knowing they'd have no customers while Vulpus was fighting. Still further below, in the bowels of the huge amphitheatre, a lion coughed irritably to itself.

'Yes. Fighting a Jew, isn't he?'

'Can't stand 'em. Stink they do. Nearly got my eye ripped out by one. Must have been . . . about the last year of old Nero. Bastard!'

He spat reflectively, idly running a finger over some of the names carved on the stone walls by men about to fight. About to die.

'Secutor, isn't he, today? Old Vulpus?'

'Yes. The Jew's a retiarius. Won't have a chance against our boy.'

'Well. . . . I know that Vulpus is good. But I always reckon a good netman'll beat a good swordman any day.'

'Venus, Decius! You wouldn't like to hazard a few . . .'

'No! No. On a Jew against Vulpus? My brains aren't all addled like some. I've seen the best and been the best, Paulus. You know that. How many men alive can boast that they once had an Emperor on his hands and knees in front of them while they rammed their . . .'

'We know. If you've told us that one about when Nero was mad as a baited bear and used to dress up like a woman and come round to get one of us to do him once, they you've told us a hundred hundred times.' He saw that Decius was about to go on, and interrupted him again. '*And* how his breath stank of leeks because he reckoned they made him sing better.'

'Aye. And he sang a merry tune while I ploughed his godlike furrow for him!'

The two old men clung to each other laughing as the main procession suddenly swept round a corner and brushed them into an alcove. Boys, maidens, slaves, Nubians, attendants of all shapes and sizes being shepherded along by the chubby figure of the chief of the arena.

And behind them came the two gladiators.

The unmistakable figure of Vulpus led the way, his face hidden under the polished helmet, the long rectangular shield slung over his shoulder. His body gleamed with oil, and even in the dim light of the corridor the two old men could see the network of pale scars that seamed his body from dozens of combats.

'Looks good, doesn't he?' whispered Decius.

'Gets better every time,' replied Paulus.

'Saw him in his second fight in Rome. Years back. Did I ever tell you about my brother?'

'Yes. He fought in the old Twentieth Legion in Britain when Vulpus's father was legate. Before the disgrace.'

Their conversation was drowned by the cheering that erupted way over their heads as the mob caught their first glimpse of their hero, the noise buffeting back down the narrow passageway to where they waited.

'Didn't think much of the look of the Jew.'

'Couldn't see much of him anyway with that great bandage over his nose.'

'That fat bestiarius broke it for him last night when he'd had too much wine. Looks strong though.'

'Five that Vulpus takes him before I count ten tens.'

'Counting right speed then, or I'll have your gizzard out of you.'

'Done. Come on, or we'll miss it all.'

Coughing and wheezing the two old men scuttled up the slope towards the arena seeing the Gate of Death grow larger straight across the sand from them as they neared the heat and stench of the amphitheatre.

The cheering was deafening.

Vulpus hardly noticed the deafening noise. Nor did he even bother to look at the man he would soon be trying to kill. He knew that it was supposed to be a Jew and that was all. It wasn't a man he'd heard of, so he didn't much care. Caring was for the dead.

The attendants left them to march alone towards the centre of the arena, turning to face the editor, leaning out of his box with a smile of anticipation that was so wide it seemed to overfill his mouth and dribble off his lips. Vulpus lifted up his sword, easing the straps of his shield on his arm. At his side the Jew lifted up his trident, the net draped carefully over his left arm.

Together they muttered the traditional words: 'Ave! Morituri te salutant!'

The editor waved a negligent hand to them and they turned again and marched away, taking up their positions facing each other across the arena. For the first time Vulpus looked up at his opponent, his eyes taking in the professional details that might make the difference between leaving the amphitheatre walking and being dragged out with a hook through his ankle.

The Jew was shorter than he was. Broad in the shoulders with a deep chest. Good fighting build. While they waited for the signal to begin he was carefully folding the net, letting the weights round the edge trail in the dirt. Dark curly hair, cropped to the nape of his neck. Great bandage over half his face. Didn't seem to interfere with his sight. Maybe one of the heavy gamblers had paid the fat bestiarius to work him over last night. It happened, and Vulpus was enough of a fatalist to know that it might even happen to him one day. So he took the chance that it could help him today.

Tomorrow would be another day for him, and another fight in a hot arena, while the crowd screamed for him. The screams were rising to a crescendo.

'Vulpus! Vulpus the Fox!! Vulpus!!!!'

He felt sweat running under his helmet, trickling down his face. One of the first tricks he'd picked up from old Argos, way back in the cold and wet of Britain, was to rub grease round your eyes to divert some of the sweat away.

The thought of Britain made him pause for a moment, still staring at his opponent. A Jew from hundreds of miles away. A prisoner, some said, who now chose to fight in the arena rather than choke his life out down a sulphur mine. And himself.

Vulpus.

The Fox.

That was what they called him, because he relied as much on his wits as on his strength to win his combats. Over the years he'd almost got used to the name, and tended to sometimes forget what he was really called.

Marcus Julius Britannicus, only son of Lucian Julius, legate of the Twentieth Legion. Mother, Elfleda, a princess of the Iceni, kin of Boadicea. The thought of his legendary great-aunt sent Marcus's sword-hand to his neck, where he wore a small pebble on a leather thong. A trinket of no worth, yet a stone handed to him by Boadicea the Queen, when he was only five years old. A skinny brat with frozen knees. A year later the Queen was dead.

Out of the corner of his eye he saw the hand of the editor drop, and the roaring of the mob all around him reached a hysterical peak and then fell away to near silence.

He put away the thoughts of twenty-two years ago, to concentrate on killing the Jew as well and as safely as he could. The past was dust on the straight road, many hills back. His father's disgrace, and death. The bloody revenge, all lay too far behind. Now was only heat and blood.

And death.

'Watch his feet and his leg muscles. Nobody can make a move without their legs, and they've got to show it. Never mind their eyes or their hands. Watch their legs!'

Argos's words were always with him. And they'd never let him down. Through the slits in his heavy helmet, he watched the legs of the Jew. The sandalled feet shifting through the gleaming sand, shuffling from side to side. The Colosseum silent now as every man and woman locked themselves into the duel that was being played out for their pleasure.

He held the shield high up against his chest, ready to use it either to parry a thrust from the Jew's trident, or to baulk a cast of the weighted net. The sword in his right hand probed at the scented air, seeking an opening in the defence of the other man.

But he was good. One of the best that Marcus had ever faced. There had been a Scythian who had nearly killed him once, but that had been in a stinking little provincial arena, and the floor had been bumpy. If he hadn't been able to land a good solid kick to the man's genitals as he'd rushed in, it would have ended there.

The hum from the crowd as the two men circled each other, neither wanting to make the first move. Marcus feinted with his sword, and the Jew hopped back easily out of reach, making a trial cast with the net as he retreated. Marcus had expected that and brushed it aside with the shield.

'Spit him, Vulpus!!' howled a voice from one of the lower boxes, and the mob yelled their approval.

There had been times when Marcus had actually seen gladiators do what the crowd shouted in an attempt to win popular approval. Most times it won them an early passage through the Gate of Death.

Again the net whistled towards him. Instead of trying to step back from it, Marcus dived under it, sword hacking for the legs of his opponent. The Jew was fast, jumping sideways, and still having time to lunge down with his long trident. Twisting like a hooked fish, Marcus managed to get his sword back and up in time to parry the blow, but it meant losing his shield, letting go of the straps and leaving it lying there uselessly in the centre of the arena.

Way above him, her face a tiny white dot among thousands of others, Poppaea almost fainted at the sight, her eyes closing and an involuntary scream passing her dry lips. The amphitheatre filled with the collective gasp of horror and shock as they saw their favourite, seemingly defenceless, still on one knee with the retiarius coming at him, swinging the weighted net like a flail.

Poppaea couldn't look.

Marcus looked up at his death closing in at him, squinting at the shadow that seemed to block off the blue sky. If he tried to parry the blow with the net with his sword arm, it would wrap round him and he would be as good as dead. There was only one thing a sensible man could do and that was to try and dive backwards, out of reach of both net and trident. That was what every single person in the crowd expected to see him do. And that was what the Jew expected as well. In anticipation he had even shifted his balance forwards slightly for the lunge.

The retiarius never wore greaves to protect his legs, as other types of gladiator did. Instead of going back, Marcus went forwards, slicing in an instant arc of steel at the Jew's leading left knee.

There were few feelings more satisfying to the gladiator than the jar running up the arm that told of a blow biting home against flesh and bone. The Jew screamed as the blade caught him at the centre of the delicate knee-joint, slicing through skin and flesh, cracking the bones, and hacking the cartilage apart. Blood splattered on the sand, the noise drowned by the roar of the crowd at the sight.

That was it. Marcus knew it was over. As the Jew had been fighting as a prisoner, his death was certain. If the crowd were well enough disposed to spare him, he would be sewn back together and sent to the mines where he might live a month.

He stepped back, holding the sword ready. His face distorted with pain, the Jew rose to his feet, levering himself up on the haft of his trident, leaving the net a twisted heap on the red sand at his feet. One end of the bandage had come loose from his nose and hung crookedly over his mouth, like a flap of white skin.

Like a crippled bird, he simply stood there, unable to move without falling, totally unable to defend himself, or to pose any threat to Marcus. There was always the possibility that a desperate retiarius might risk all on a throw of the three-pronged trident, but the Jew couldn't even balance himself to stand, and could never throw.

It was over.

The crowd knew it, and screamed at their hero to go in and make the kill. Marcus had guessed that a Jew would never be spared. There were those with long enough memories in Rome to recall the rising in Jerusalem and the slaughter at Masada, the fortress of rock.

Panting with the heat and the tension, Marcus was enough of a professional to know that the stocky opponent had come closer to killing him than any man. Now he waited patiently, blood flowing from his crippling wound, for Marcus to come in again and end it. He had never even bothered to appeal to the mob, content, seemingly, with his lot. Then again, these Jews were always a proud, unbending race.

Marcus reached up and tore off his padded helmet, feeling the air cooler on his face, looking to the box for the sign from the editor, though he knew what it would be. No candidate for high office would be fool enough to go against the baying of the tiers and spare the man after they'd howled for his life.

There was a moment of quiet as every eye turned to the young man in the main box, still sitting with his arm round a lady who some said was not his cousin. Marcus heard a muffled exclamation from behind him, and turned round. The Jew was staring at his face as though he saw the ghost of one of his ancestors.

Then the editor stood up and made a great production of leaning forward and dropping his thumb in the signal for death. The crowd cheered him, broadening the smile even more.

But Marcus saw none of this.

His eyes were looking back at the Jew. His dark brown eyes gazed at Marcus, a rueful smile at the corner of his lips. Many men had faced death at Marcus's hands. Some had wept and called on their mothers. Most had simply looked at him resignedly, knowing that there was nothing that could alter the cast of the Fates. But none had ever smiled.

It seemed to Marcus as though the two of them were trapped in time. Frozen in a crystal moment, like flies in a pearl of clear honey. Isolated from the noise and the heat of the Colosseum.

Still smiling, the Jew lifted one hand from the haft of the trident and began to peel away the cloth wound over his broken nose.

Until his face was revealed.

All about them the mob were standing and shrieking for their hero to strike and slay the loser so that all bets could be settled up and they could go home well satisfied. But their Vulpus still stood there and looked at the Jew, hanging crippled on his weapon, a pool of red sand about his feet.

At the mouth of the corridor, Decius had slowed his count as far as he could, but he finally reached the tenth ten, and stopped, cursing Vulpus.

'Stick him, Vulpus!'

Poppaea wondered if her idol was prolonging the wait to make the wretch suffer all the more. The idea excited her and her busy little fingers moused under gown and burrowed deep again.

Oblivious to all this, Marcus stood, sword hanging at his side, staring at the face of the Jew.

Shaking sweat from his face, the wounded man grinned at him. 'Aye. It is Samuel ben Ezra. No ghost.' He paused. 'Yet. Come, brother. Strike. I have had enough of debts.'

Still Marcus made no move.

A last time the Jew spoke. 'Strike, brother. I am the enemy you must kill, my friend.'

TWO

Samuel ben Ezra. Marcus's mind flashed back from the Colosseum in the first year of the Emperor Domitian. Back from the heat of Imperial Rome to the sticky heat of Jerusalem.

How many years ago? Nine? Ten? It was in the fourth year of Vespasian. And Marcus had been a youth of only seventeen summers.

His mind went back.

'Do you only have these miserable little sextarii of this stinking camel piss you call wine?'

Marcus Julius Britannicus was very drunk. Otherwise he would never have gone into the small wine-shop on his own. Even at seventeen he knew better than that. But there had been this slim, dark-eyed slut who had sidled up to him out of one of the narrow side-streets that still stood from the sacking of the city two years before. Her lips were warm and her body seemed willing under a thin woollen dress.

General Titus had expelled most of the Jews from the city after he had destroyed their temple in an attempt to finally end the four-year revolt of the Zealots. Now they were creeping back again and the place was beginning to seem more like it had once been. The only difference was that the Romans were there in massive force.

With a wave of her hand the girl called over a man with another half-litre of their red wine. Silver bracelets jingled on her wrists as she moved. And she wore tiny silver bells through the lobes of her ears that tinkled whenever she shook her head or laughed. Marcus thought that laughter was one of the sweetest sounds he had ever heard.

It had been early evening when they'd come in. He could

vaguely remember that the alleys were getting dark, and that the harsh clatter of marching feet meant the curfew was approaching. For any soldier not to be either in camp or on active duty after that time would mean, at best, a flogging that would bare his backbone to the lash.

But Marcus was in an almost unique position. He was of the Tenth Legion but not directly within it. That anomaly had arisen because of a whim of the officer commanding the Legion. An old friend of Marcus's father – Flavius Silva.

The girl excused herself for some reason – Marcus didn't quite catch what she said – leaving him alone with the flagon of wine and a rough glass standing in its own pool of sticky red liquid. He tried to stretch his eyelids to take away the odd feeling of heaviness, but they remained sore, as though someone had blown hot sand into them. He clutched the half-full glass, slurping wine over the wood, gazing miserably into it, suddenly feeling very alone.

The General had taken him on as a sort of auxiliary scout, despite the objections of some of the younger officers about having the son of the traitor in their Legion. Flavius Silva had called a few of those well-connected young aristocrats into his tent and spoken with them in private for some time. After that there had been no obvious slights to Marcus, but he knew better than to try and fight them all. So he kept his place and held his tongue.

And he was eternally grateful to Flavius Silva for giving him the chance to avenge his father's name. He knew well enough that the stories that had led to his father's suicide were false. But his mother *had* been Britain-born. He might be a free-born Roman as far as the law was concerned, but there would always be that stigma. The manner of his mother's rejection and the lonely, shameful death of his father rose before him, and he nearly vomited up the cheap wine, feeling the bitter taste of bile in his mouth.

'What's wrong with you, my little dove?' asked the girl, with heavy solicitousness, bending over him, letting her hand fall near his sword. 'Why don't you take that nasty thing off, and then maybe you and me could go upstairs and get to be really good friends.'

'Good friends!' He stood up, knocking her arm from him.

Drunk he might be, and only a boy, but no one touched his sword, unless it would be to remove it from his corpse and return it to his mother, alone in the northern mists.

Shaking his head to try and clear the dust from his brain, peering round the smoky hovel. Lamps burning oily fat gave a dim red glow, and he suddenly realized that the place was filling up. Silently, in ones and twos, there were more than a dozen men there. All keeping quiet. All Jews by the look of them.

Had he been a little more drunk he would have staggered away. Had he been a little less drunk, he would have seen the risk he ran and left.

Either way, he might have been a dead man before he crossed the threshold. As it was, Marcus simply removed them from his mind and sat down again. Laying his head on the table, feeling the lees of wine sticking to the fuzz of his sprouting beard.

'Is my face not like the rising sun?' he asked, giggling at the girl. He tried to smile an even bigger smile, so that his face would grow redder and rounder, and then she would see what he meant.

'Like the setting sun of Rome,' someone said. A young man, near his age as far as he could judge, sitting alone in a shadowed alcove.

'Hold your tongue, boy,' spat another, older man. Adding something in what sounded to Marcus's befuddled mind like the Hebrew language.

'Yes. Yes. You hold your tongue, boy, or I'll have some of the lads from the good old Tenth come and hold it for you. With red-hot irons.'

It seemed a fine jest, and he tried to repeat it, but it slipped away from him. The room also appeared to have shrunk, and was revolving solemnly about his ears. There was a ring of faces watching him. And the boy – the one in the corner – was talking to them. Trying to convince them of something. But he was being argued down.

Losing interest in what was going on, he took another gulp of the wine, and stared at the girl. 'You've got a lot of friends, haven't you? I don't have many. As you were. I don't have any. I'm always alone. That's me. Poor old Marcus Julius Britannicus.'

There was a Legion marching song about never being on your own while you had your weapons and your friends. There was the sound of marching feet outside, stopping for a moment. Marcus looked up, watching as the ring of men dissolved from close to him and went and replaced itself round the edge of the room. The feet went away again as he tried to beat time with the wineglass.

'I'm doing well,' he muttered. Until the glass broke into jagged shards, the razored edges glinting back with the red glow of the lamps. He smiled foolishly as he saw a small worm of blood creeping from between the fingers of his right hand, and he raised his hand to his mouth and licked at it, enjoying the salt taste.

One of the older men said something to the girl, and gestured upstairs. She looked at him, and replied in a low voice. The noise reminded him of geese gobbling away on his uncle's farm in the hills a couple of days' ride from Rome, and Marcus laughed.

'Tell the old pimp that I'm ready to take you upstairs right now and that I shall perform my drill with all the skill of a Roman officer and patrician. And pay the reckoning as well.'

Another splutter of gobbling from the men to the girl, and then she smiled at him and took his arm, helping him to his feet. He made a clumsy bow to the rest of the men, including the dark youth in the alcove. For a moment it seemed to him that the boy was going to speak to him, but the moment passed and he allowed himself to be led to the rickety wooden stairs.

'Sure you don't want to leave that pig-sticker behind you, my little love?'

Marcus risked a joke with the Jewish girl. 'I keep that weapon ready for anything. And I've got another weapon ready to show you.'

'I'm sure you have, my bold little hawk,' grinned the girl, putting her arm round his shoulders. 'And I shall be glad to see it.'

At the top of the steps there was a narrow landing, looking down into the main room of the wineshop. Marcus paused by the flimsy rail and peered down. The men had moved from the walls to the centre and all sat around a table talking animatedly. All except the boy, who seemed to have vanished. As one of them saw Marcus blinking owlishly at them, he muttered something to the rest, then called up to the young Roman. Marcus couldn't understand what he said, and turned to the girl.

'He says that he hopes that you have a sound sleep, my brave lover.'

With a cheerful wave, he acknowledged the words, but the effort of standing there, with the heat of the room billowing round him, was almost too much and he staggered and nearly fell.

'By Mithras! This heat is worse than Rome in the middle of day.'

'It is always hot in the month of Elul,' said the girl.

'Is that the same as August in your tongue?' he asked as she pushed him into a tiny room. Unfurnished but for a bed and a small chair. A square window high up one wall was the only way out.

Her nimble fingers began to unpin her dress, letting it fall to the floor in a whisper of sound. 'Aye. August to you Romans. Elul to us of the Chosen People. And the word is Gorpiaeus in the tongue of the Syrians and Macedonians.'

Marcus wore the short tunic that most young men of his age preferred, but he also wore a skirt of metal strips, and carried his short sword in a scabbard dangling from a broad leather belt. The only light for the room came from a small lamp stuck half-way up the wall on a dab of dried clay. It smoked and stank abominably, but he had little concern for it.

The girl casually kicked her dress across the dirt floor so that it lay against the chair. Reaching behind her she pushed the door closed until the latch clicked shut.

'There, my fine young man. Now we're all alone and there's nobody going to come and interrupt us. Why don't you show me this great weapon you were boasting of down below. Or d'you think the very sight of it might frighten me into a faint?'

She wasn't the first woman Marcus had ever seen naked. Not by a long way. There'd been slave-girls, and whores in every camp. Women that a man used for the purpose that the Gods had made them for. For most soldiers, the camp-followers were there to be used as and when needed. And when they could afford them. The act had little more meaning than the daily visit to the latrine trench.

Marcus had always looked at them with a touch more care. His father had taught him to respect free-born women of any tribe, and only to use slave-girls when he felt he had to. But the women who trailed over the land after the Legions were different from this one. They were fat old whores, often in their thirties. They simply lay back and let the men spend themselves between their sagging thighs while they yawned or munched on an apple with their toothless jaws.

But this one. This . . . he realized that he didn't even know her name.

'What are you called?'

'Many things, my hawk. You may call me Judith.' She stood close before him and cupped her breasts, holding them up towards him, so that the nipples stood out like the summer cherries of the mountain pastures, topping mounds of fresh pastry, ready for the baking.

'Nibble on my fruits, Roman,' she teased him, reaching under the short tunic, her fingers cupping him through the thin cotton of his undergarments, finding him ready and aroused. 'So! That is indeed a mighty weapon, and I fear me that you will split me in twain. Come, my little boy with your great sword. Take off your clothes and lie with me, and we will see what we can do together.'

Smiling at her, trying to hold his face from slipping apart into a grin of idiot vacuity, Marcus fumbled with the brooch that held his tunic together, letting it drop so that he was naked to the waist. The girl lay back on the bed, spreading her legs, touching herself and whispering to him. Promising him nameless delights. Telling him of how they might twine and move, one under the other. Offering him her body to hook and probe into. To thrust against.

And all the time he felt that his loins were near to bursting with his desire for her. He caught a nail on the heavy buckle of his belt, and cursed. At the back of his mind was the shameful fear that he might be sick in front of this woman. The belt was new, and he had pulled it tight around him before he left the camp that afternoon. Judith's movements became more abandoned, and he finally gave it up, and simply pulled off his drawers, leaving his belt on and his sword still in its sheath.

The girl gazed up at him, seeing a young man in the full flush of his first strength. Taller than most men she had known, with broad shoulders and a deep chest that spoke of great power. Dark hair, black rather than brown, cut short in a fringe at the front in the Roman manner, and longer at the back, hanging straight down over the nape of his muscular neck. Brown eyes, unusual among the men from the west that she had seen over the years.

The long years of Roman rule. Before they had finally broken down the mighty temple of Jerusalem and ravaged the city as a warning to the Zealots who had dared to revolt. All that now stood were the towers of Phasaelus, Hippicus and Mariamne, and the wall that enclosed what was left of the city on the west side. It was on this side, hard against the wall, that the Tenth Legion were camped.

'Your sword!' For the first time there was a definite edge to her voice, and it penetrated even through Marcus's drink-fuddled brain.

'I shall keep it on. Whether you like or no. Would you wish me to go?'

Judith saw her error and tried to make up for it, getting off the bed and coming to him, pulling his body to her. Touching him, and kissing him, pressing her lips to his, her tongue probing like a small serpent between his teeth. Marcus gave himself over to her at first, until he became aware that the sweetness of her fire was tainted with corruption, like a fly-blown peach.

She sensed that the mood was slipping away from him, and fell back on the bed, dragging him on top of her, taking his fingers and making him touch her, deep in the warm dampness among the wiry hair. Closing her thighs on his wrist and undulating her stomach muscles so that he might respond to her readiness.

'Quickly, my lover. Before I burst with my passion for you. Quickly! Or would you rather have it the Greek way?'

The sword pommel was sticking into his hip and Marcus rolled over to his side, breaking free for a moment from her sucking grasp. Her words and her body had combined to make him forget any reservations he might have had, and he pushed the belt round out of the way, lowering himself between her spread thighs, as she used her hand to guide him deep within her. Gasping, feeling the sickness beginning to rise again, Marcus thrust brutally at her, while she ground her hips against him, rising to meet every lunge.

He'd learned very early in life that the act of coupling with a woman was often made more pleasurable if he could hold back from his own climax, and he gritted his teeth, forcing back both his lust and his rising sickness. The bed shook and rattled, and his sword banged against the wooden frame, making a noisy accompaniment to their lovemaking.

'Please take it off and lay it by the door, Roman. It drowns my pleasure with its clattering.'

Grunting with irritation, Marcus eased himself off her, wincing at the sucking noise as their sweat-soaked bodies broke apart. He was really beginning to wonder if all this was worth it, and he was also beginning to sober up a little. The reality of his position began to creep out of the small room at the back of his mind where he'd managed to lock it during the evening, and it was an uncomfortable thought. A lone Roman, in a wine-shop, coupling with a Jewish woman, while a dozen or more Jews waited down the stairs.

There'd been cases of soldiers on their own being found the next morning in some stinking alley with their throat gaping open and their privates hacked off and stuck in their mouth. Feeling an odd chill, Marcus shivered.

'Cold, my sweetheart?'

'Or someone walking over my grave,' he replied, standing undecided near the door. Unconsciously, his fingers crept to his lucky stone and stroked it.

'Come on to bed, lover, and I'll soon warm you up again. Come on.'

There was a biting edge to her voice that helped sober Marcus up quicker than the morning bark of an angry centurion. Something was wrong.

'What'll it cost me to lie with you, Jewess? Answer me that.'

'A handsome boy like you! Tell you what; I normally do ask a small gift in return, maybe a denarius or two, but I'll do it for nothing, seeing as I like you. Now come to bed and leave your sword over there.'

'Is that all the price?'

'That, and your throat expertly cut.'

The woman gasped at the new voice. A soft voice, hardly rising above a whisper. Coming from the small window.

Marcus looked up, trying to see who it was, his sword hissing from its sheath. All he could see was a dark face, blocking out the pale moonlight.

'Roman. If you want to see your city again, you'd do well to stick that whore before she screams and brings all of her friends up here. Though I fear they may already be on the way here.'

It was a warning he didn't need. It was as though he'd never been drunk. Fear dropped a cold curtain over his mind, clearing it and sharpening his reflexes. He noticed that the noise of talk from down the stairs had stopped, and the place was as silent as a tomb. At the same time he saw Judith trying to roll off the bed the other side, mouth already opening for a scream.

Like a panther he leaped on top of her, digging his knee into her soft stomach, driving the air from her lungs in a whoosh of pain and shock. The sword-point went between her breasts, the tip drawing a bead of blood that ran slowly over her dark stomach, vanishing in her mat of pubic hair.

'One sound, you dung-hill slut, and by Mithras it will be your last!'

There was a creak from outside the room door as though someone was trying to climb the stairs in silence and not making a good job of it.

'Quickly, Roman. Or you're a dead man.' The whisper was softer, as though the man outside had moved a little away from the window.

'We are all dead men, given a little span of life by the Gods. Remember that, Jew.' His whispered reply carried to the man, and he was rewarded by an almost inaudible laugh.

Marcus sat cautiously back on the woman's stomach, keeping his sword braced against her body, holding her flat on the bed. The squeaking had stopped from the landing, but he was sure there was someone there.

Just for a moment he hesitated, trying to weigh up all the odds, and finding them too heavily against him. The way out had to be through that tiny window. To try for it while the woman was there meant that she would call for help and he would be hacked down while he struggled out. And there was no way he could silence her without making a noise.

So?

He leaned quickly forward, placing one hand firmly over her mouth, and put his weight behind the sword point. It went in like a skewer into a joint of well-hung meat, sinking into her stomach without a sound. Marcus felt her body tense with the shock and agony, then he twisted the broad blade so that it tore her lungs and heart apart in one savage movement, killing her instantly.

Her back arched, almost throwing him off, and her teeth clenched on his palm, nearly making him cry out with the pain. Blood trickled from her nostrils, and her eyes protruded from her head like someone who'd been strangled. Marcus swung himself off her, noticing with a passing interest that her nipples had again become erect.

He drew out his sword and wiped it on the stained blanket, using her discarded dress to mop the gouts of dark blood from his own stomach and thighs. Picked up his clothes and slipped quickly into them, finding that his fingers trembled ever so slightly as he did up the brooch on his tunic.

'Quickly!'

The voice was urgent. Marcus looked at the naked corpse, blood trickling to the dirty floor, the stomach and chest a gaping wound. He felt in his tunic and pulled out a handful of small bronze coins. Asses, the lowest denomination of currency. He took three or four and threw them among the wreck of Judith's body.

'All you were worth to me,' he muttered, eyeing the high window and wondering if he could make it without being heard.

The decision was further complicated by a whisper. This time it came not from his unknown friend outside the window but from outside the door.

'Judith. Judith! Is all well?'

The door opened inwards, and Marcus stepped silently across and eased up the wooden peg that acted as a latch. Sword ready in his hand, he suddenly jerked the flimsy door open, and lunged at the figure he saw crouching there. The Jewish assassin had no chance at all, taken completely by surprise by the savage attack. The sword hit home under his left arm, snapping ribs into splinters of bone, the power of the blow sending him staggering back against the balustrade. He was a short man, heavily built, wearing a dark blue cloak. His weight was enough to smash the rail, and he teetered for a second on the brink, arms flapping at empty air. But the wound was mortal and he lacked the strength to pull himself back from the brink. With a cry of fear and despair, he plunged from Marcus's sight, the cloak floating about him like the wings of some huge bat. There was a great crash as he landed on the table below, and a roar of pain from someone injured by his body.

'Come, you Jewish rats!!' roared Marcus at the top of his voice, hoping the noise might attract one of the frequent foot patrols. 'Kill me while I lay with your whore! Come and face me now!'

There was a moment of silence, and then a voice giving orders in their own tongue. From behind him, Marcus heard the scrabbling noise of someone trying to climb in through the small window, and glanced round, fearing for his back. But his eyes met the grinning face of the young man who had been sitting in the alcove, holding a small dagger in each hand, joining him on the narrow landing.

'I have no love for Romans, but I like less the curs who stab in the back.'

Down below their enemies were gathering, pushing at one another, as no man wished to be the first up the stairs. Marcus smiled at his ally. 'I have no love for Jews, but I call a man friend who stands with me in such a place as this. I am in your debt, brother. I am called Marcus Julius Britannicus.'

'And I Samuel ben Ezra. Guard yourself!!'

The killers below had finally worked up their courage and made a dash at the stairs, led by the bearded fellow who had called out earlier. He had a long sword in his hand, and he lunged at Marcus before he'd even reached the top of the stairs. That was a grave error. In fighting with swords, there was a great advantage with the man standing as Marcus did. Higher and immovable. The landing gave him a firm base to move easily, parrying the Jew's thrust, and counter quickly with a cut to the side of the man's face that opened a wound streaming blood from forehead to chin.

He screamed, and dropped his weapon, clasping his fingers to the bleeding gash. With the speed and efficiency of a ritual slaughterer, Marcus neatly lopped through his left arm, nearly slicing the man's head from his broad shoulders. A foot in the chest and the corpse toppled back among his fellows, knocking another of them off his feet.

'Neatly done, Roman. Ezekiel was a doughty fighter among us.'

'Then you are sadly lacking in men of skill, Jew, if he was the best you had to offer.'

The next attack was better prepared, and it nearly ended the fight there and then. Two of them came together, both using captured Roman javelins. Biting at the air before them, weaving a net of death that Marcus couldn't break, and he was forced back until he stood up against the young Jew.

He was about to launch a desperate counter-attack against them, and try to drive them from their perilous fortress, when he heard a whisper.

'Move to your left, brother.'

Knocking away a lunge from one of the javelins that had threatened to gut him, Marcus hopped to one side, giving Samuel ben Ezra the chance to use one of his knives. With a lightning overhand throw, he sent his blade spinning at the face of one of the attackers.

It was well aimed.

It thudded into his eye-socket with a sickly sound, sticking there like some hideous ornament. Clear fluid spurted from the wound, followed by pale blood. The man's body went as stiff as a board, and he dropped the spear, toppling forward at Marcus's feet, his hand still trembling, fingers scratching at the wood. Though the knife had pierced clear through the eye into his brain and killed him instantly.

Marcus didn't pause to watch the death throes, leaping over the twitching body to hack down the other Jew with the javelin. As his sword plunged into his enemy's stomach, his left hand reached out and grabbed the spear from the nerveless fingers. A push and a wrench of the blade, and there was a fifth corpse in the small wine-shop.

And there was the sound of running feet in the cobbled alley outside.

'The Legion!' hissed ben Ezra behind him. 'Once they get in here, there will be a great killing.'

The Jews below had also heard the pounding of the soldiers' sandals, and made a last attack. But they already knew the attempt was doomed, and that they had picked on a stray mouse and found it had turned into a ravening lion. There was little enthusiasm for the charge. Nobody wanted to be the first up those shivering steps to face the grim-faced youth and his unexpected ally.

One fellow finally screwed up his courage and made the try, only to fall back with the javelin point protruding a hand's-span through his shoulder-blades and blood gushing from his mouth, drowning his last scream.

There was a pounding on the door of the wine-shop, and a harsh voice calling out for them to open in the name of the Emperor Vespasian of Rome. Marcus leaned as far out over the landing as he dared and shouted to the soldiers: 'To me, men of the Tenth! To your brother!! There is treachery here!!'

'They'll creep out the back way, and be far from here by the time your comrades break down that door,' said the young Jew at his back.

'There's a door at the rear. Watch it and take them all!' called Marcus, hearing a cry of assent from the men at the front.

A thin column of smoke began to rise from the floor below them, showing that the Zealots had fired the building to try and cover their escape. The crackling of flames told the two young men that the blaze must already have taken a fast hold on the dry timbers and tables of the small building. Even as they looked at each other the smoke grew like a great column of darkness, billowing around them, making them cough and choke.

'The window back there, brother, or we will end as roasts of meat,' said ben Ezra.

'Aye, and quickly, lest we be sadly overdone when they reach us,' replied Marcus, leading the way through the sudden blackness.

In the smoke, Marcus could scarcely see across the small bedroom, with its guttering lamp. In his haste, he tripped over the bed and fell full-length on top of Judith's corpse, beslobbering himself with her warm blood. Then he was under the window, and the air was a little cleaner. He could even manage to see a few stars winking away over his head.

Somewhere below them, there was the sound of shouting and cursing. Steel clashing against steel and the cries of wounded and dying men. The Tenth had obviously blocked the hole before the rats had found time to escape. A hand on Marcus's shoulder told him that Samuel had arrived through the smoke.

'Brother. Your friends have done all that is needful below. I would not linger to talk with them. To a Roman legionary, all Jews are Zealots. And all Zealots must be killed.'

'No friends, Samuel ben Ezra. Comrades, perhaps. Yet I think what you say is right, and it might go hard, even with my word to support you. These flat roofs all wind about one another. It should not be hard to slip away, after I have gone down and told them that there are no more dogs in this burning kennel.'

There was a pause, while Marcus leaped with an agile grace and wriggled through the small square opening, finding himself on a flat roof. Flames were dancing from the ground floor, casting a shifting light over the night. He could hear men calling out, and saw a couple of soldiers backing one of the Jews into a corner of the small courtyard, finally both spitting him, and kicking the body as it rolled about in the dirt.

There was a gasp from behind him, and Samuel joined him in the night, bending down and rubbing his leg.

'My ankle. Twisted it. Still, I can stand, so I'll be able to run.'

It was lighter there than it had been inside, and Marcus was able to see the youth for the first time. In some ways he was very like Marcus. The same tall, powerful build. Same colour hair, though Samuel's was more curly, and the same brown eyes. They were clearly of an age. Marcus guessed that the Jew was perhaps a year the older.

'You must go. One of the soldiers might see you up here. Go.' He held out his hand and the young man clasped it, in the Roman way, grasping Marcus by the wrist. 'I am in your debt, my brother. I hope that there will be a way that I can repay it. If the Zealots allow me life enough to meet you again.'

'It may be so,' said Samuel, his Roman speech surprisingly

unaccented. 'Though I spared your life here, I may not do so again, with the same ease.'

'Why?' Marcus paused on the edge of the roof, ready to leap down.

'Because, my brother from Rome, I am one of those Zealots myself.'

There was a flash of white teeth, gleaming red in the light of the fire, as he saw the look of shock on Marcus's face when he realized that his life had been saved by one of the sect that were sworn enemies of Rome. The group that had been waging war against the Imperial might for several years, now near to defeat, but for a handful of them that still fought on in some rocky fastness some forty miles south of Jerusalem.

Near the Dead Sea. The name slipped away from Marcus as he waved a quick farewell to Samuel, vanishing into the night over the roofs. Then it came back to him.

The fortress was called Masada.

THREE

'Masada!'

'Aye, lad. That's what the orders are. Seems the Jews out there are still holding on, and they need a few more brave young men to winkle them out.'

The officer was the Princeps Centurion of the Legion. Not a man to argue with, unless you wanted to endure one of the varying range of field punishments. But Marcus liked and respected the man, and he in turn admired the spirit of the boy, despite what some of the tribunes talked of over their evening meal about Marcus's father.

'They've held it for years. Why not starve them out, or just assault it and drive them off?'

'Well enough, Marcus Britannicus. They took it from some of our lads about six years back. And they're still there. That's why the Emperor, may the Gods smile on the old bastard, sent the Tenth along, with our poxy General, Flavius Silva, to try and send them running.'

'And?'

'And they're still there. Damn their eyes! When you get there in a few days, you'll see why. It's like the back side of Vulcan's arse. Hotter than anything you've ever known. More difficult to climb than a Vestal's thighs. Damn near impossible to take, I'd say.'

'Never thought I'd hear you say anything was impossible to the First Cohort of the Tenth Legion.'

'Not impossible, laddie. *Nearly* impossible. Time you get there old Flavius'll probably have it all wrapped up in a neat package.'

'I go straight there?'

The officer smiled. He was effectively one of the most senior officers of the Legion. A professional soldier, unlike the Legate and the Tribunes, all of whom were political appointments, made by the Emperor. The Centurions were the men who knew about fighting, and knew the men under their command.

Each Legion consisted of around six thousand men, split into the Cohorts, and then into Centuries. Each Century was split yet again into about eight ten men units called Contubernia. Then there were the auxiliary troops, who were rarely free-born Romans. More often they were natives, who had joined up with the army to fight for twenty-five years, when they would be released and given land *and* the great prize of citizenship.

For a Roman to choose to fight among the auxiliaries was so rare as to cause comment. Yet that was what Marcus had done, refusing the chance of rising through the ranks, and preferring to serve under his father's old and loyal friend as an auxiliary scout.

In some ways, he was a free agent. Free to either obey or disobey the orders of the grizzled veteran. Yet he knew well enough how valuable the patronage of Flavius Silva was to him – a friendless youth with a dishonoured father. And so he listened to his orders as carefully as the newest recruit in the bottom-most Cohort.

'No, Marcus. You don't quite go straight there. You know the Tribune, Flavius Julius Germanicus?'

Marcus did. He was one of the youngest of the political officers of the Legion. A gross fat man, barely thirty, whose military knowledge was limited to complaining about the food he was served. But it was alleged that he had once done Vespasian a favour. Some said the favour hadn't been unconnected with a daughter. A daughter who mysteriously vanished from the family and was supposed to have died of a fever while on holiday on the Mediterranean.

'Well. The capon wants his wife brought to see what wonders he's doing for his Emperor. She's at a camp about two days' ride from here. I want you to take an escort and bring her back. Lighten all our hearts, Marcus.'

'What's she like?'

'Well. How can I put it to you? Can you imagine a corner piss-pot on legs? Smothered in bear-grease with legs like wine kegs. They say she's built like a triumphal arch, down where it matters. I've heard that after you've put it in, you can still find room to get both hands in and . . . but then again, Marcus, I keep forgetting you're only a lad. And that your father was a Legate himself.'

To Marcus's surprise, the Centurion seemed almost to be embarrassed, as though he felt he'd gone too far with his bawdy jests. Yet they were commonplace in the Army. When mighty Julius Caesar marched in his triumphs, the songs sung about him by his own troops were so scurrilous and bawdy that respectable matrons ran screaming from the streets, covering up their ears at the language.

'Collect her, and bring her straight back here? Anyone with her?'

'Half a dozen servants, I suppose. And there's a couple of merchants. Bought their citizenships, and they're coming here to this stinking place yelling they want an escort in case the Zealots get to them and cut off their precious ... supplies. Or something.'

Marcus turned away from the Centurion, ready to leave his tent, when the officer called him back. 'One other thing about the Lady Agrippina.'

'What?'

'Don't get on the wrong side of her. Whatever I say about her, the bitch has a lot of power. Her brother is an influential man. As much as Flavius Silva. He's your protection at the moment, and he's high in favour. But if he fails to take Masada for Vespasian ...'

He let the sentence tail off.

'If he fails ...?'

'Then you're going to need all the friends you can get, young Marcus Julius Britannicus.'

The Centurion had been right. The Lady Agrippina Germanicus was very conscious of her position and of her family connections. By the time that Marcus arrived with a party of cavalry to collect her, the camp where she'd been was utterly sick of her. She complained that he was late, and made some of the nastiest threats he'd heard outside of the Praefectus Castrorum – as the senior Centurion was called – when someone fainted at a big parade.

And she lived up to the description of her.

Hardly had Marcus dismounted when she demanded that he be brought to her. It was sweltering hot in the small house she had procured for herself, and she was reclining on a long couch, while a small native boy cooled her with a fan of white feathers. She wore a gown of faded yellow, trimmed with the thin strip of purple, and she was eating from a plate of sweetmeats and gulping from a green goblet of wine.

She was fat, but not quite as appalling as the Centurion had made out. True enough, small black bristles, like those of a rutting hog, sprouted from her nostrils, but Marcus found her not ill-favoured.

Her voice was a constant whine. Why was he late? Why was he so young? Why hadn't the general come to meet her? How was her dear husband? Was it this hot at Jerusalem? Were the Zealots really a danger? How many men did he have?

Marcus did his best to reassure her that there was little danger of their being attacked, as the uprising had nearly been suppressed, with only the one pocket of resistance left to be crushed. Agrippina seemed happier, and called him over to sit beside her, slapping irritably at the boy with the fan to get him to work harder.

'So idle, these people. You know, Marcus Britannicus ... I may call you that, may I not? Yesterday, I had to whip one of my girls for being late with my food. And the baggage had the nerve to scream at the top of her voice all the time. It set me to weeping, she went on for so long. In the end it became quite unbearable, and I told her that I'd have her tongue pulled out if she made any more noise. Of course, that shut her up.'

During the story, she had sat up and edged along the couch, towards Marcus, holding out the dish of sweetmeats for him. Patting him on the arm for refusing. It seemed to the youth that it was getting hotter, and he ran a finger round the neck of his tunic to try and cool himself. Agrippina noticed the gesture, and wiped his forehead with a large red hand.

'Poor boy. It is desperately warm in here, is it not? I wear nothing at all under this gown, you know, and I am still hot.'

Truth to tell, she was sweating in rivers, and the oppressive smell of her body was making Marcus yearn for the cleaner air outside. But he bore in mind the words of his officer and forced a smile for her. Her patting hand had reached his thigh, when he stood up quickly.

'Your pardon, my lady, but there is much to attend to before we leave at first light on the morrow.' He saw the look of disappointment on her face. 'Perhaps, before I leave your presence, I might sample one of those small cakes, to keep the memory with me of your beauty.'

It was a clumsy compliment, but Agrippina simpered at it, smiling up at him with moist eyes. 'Naughty boy. Such talk to a respectable married lady. If my husband were to hear you talk in such a way! Still, you are young, and I forgive you. Here.'

She offered him the tray, overflowing with small pastries. Marcus ran his eye quickly over them, seeing they were the usual mixture of plums, cherries, quinces, nuts and apples, baked in little boats and soaked in honey. He picked one out at random, and popped it into his mouth, watched by the lady's hungry eyes.

'There. Wasn't that excellent?'

Mumbling through a mouthful of pastry crumbs, Marcus muttered his agreement.

'I always say, that there is nothing like a nibble of something as the afternoon wears on. Would you not agree, Marcus Britannicus?'

'Indeed, my lady?' His answer became a question, as he saw her face change. 'What's wrong?'

'Marcus Julius Britannicus. Was your father not Lucian Julius?'

The friendship, and much else besides, had slipped from her face, and she looked at him suspiciously. A look that Marcus had learned to recognize over the last years.

'He was, my lady. And it was he who married the princess of the Iceni. And who was accused of treason, and though there was no evidence against him, chose to end his life in the way of honour.'

He rattled it off, as he had before, to check the painful and embarrassed way men and women questioned him when they suspected who his family were.

Agrippina stood up, looking at him as though he were the representative of some alien race. 'And Flavius Silva trusts you with an errand of this importance?'

'Indeed. Have no fear, my lady. You will be as safe with me as with any other.' He bowed and walked to the doorway of the room, then turned, unable to resist a last shaft. 'That is, if the Zealots don't come down at us.'

Marcus smiled at the gasp, and walked back to join his men feeling better than he had for some time.

The next morning he went with half a dozen troops to inspect their transport, taking up most of the time with bargaining with a trader of horses for some sorry-looking nags. Finally losing patience, Marcus took the man on one side and rested his hand on the silver hilt of his sword.

'My friend. If I were to think you a spy for the Jews, and if you tried to escape from my examination, and if I were to cut you down . . . then there would be little said, and your goods would be forfeit to Rome.'

The little dealer looked up at the brown eyes of the youth, even younger than his own son, and he shuddered. Used though he was to threats and to dealing with men of authority, there was something to this boy that sent a chill down his spine, and made his fingers shake. Some depth of ruthlessness that made him believe implicitly that he would do what he had threatened.

'Do you understand me, horse-trader?'

'Aye, lord. Right well. You make your meaning as clear as the finest crystal glass. You shall have the mounts at the price you last offered.'

Marcus smiled. 'No. I shall have the horses for one half of what I last offered, and be glad that I do not slit your scrawny throat to seal the bargain.'

And so it was done, and they trotted slowly back to the camp, along the silent streets of the tiny town to where the rest of the party were waiting. As he swung off his horse's back, Marcus heard the noise of raised voices, coming from the small square at the back of the house where the Lady Agrippina was ensconced. Women's voices. Angry, and shrill.

Quickly knotting the reins round a post, Marcus ran round the corner of the building, his sword out ready in his hand in case of trouble. Finding the trouble was merely a quarrel between Agrippina and the skinny wife of one of the merchants, whose name he didn't even know. All he had noticed was that she made every effort to ape the manners of the Roman patrician class, and never quite got it right. Her clothes and her appearance *just* missed being correct, and she knew it. It was truly said that one could dress an ape in the purple of the Emperor, and he would yet remain an ape.

Admittedly, that had been said many years ago, and in a different context, but it was still true.

'Just because your brother happens once to have kissed the backside of the Emperor, you think that makes you someone important. Well, I can tell you, mistress, that all those fine words of yours don't make you any better.'

Agrippina stood with her hands on her hips, glaring at the smaller woman. 'You shrew! Better a husband who makes his career as mine does, than a jumped-up native plebeian who made his fortune from selling bad vinegar to the army.'

'Bad vinegar!!'

'Bad vinegar!!!'

For a moment, Marcus thought that the two ladies were about to hurl themselves at each other like a couple of whores from the Via Cloaca, but the merchant's wife just managed to keep control of herself.

'You think the army's that wonderful, Lady Agrippina Germanicus? Well, see if you can get a man from that stinking rabble you call an escort, under that beardless traitor's son, and let them stand against my husband's man, Atilus, in mortal combat.'

Agrippina saw Marcus standing, white-faced, watching them, and realized that he must have heard everything that had just been said. Her manner at their previous meeting had made it clear that she felt like the others about the generosity of the General in helping the son of a man who was supposed to have betrayed his country. Yet she had enough respect for Rome and for her laws, that she was prepared to accept Marcus as the officer in charge of her escort.

'My dear Marcus! Did you hear what this woman has been saying about you?'

He schooled his face to reflect none of his anger and bitterness, making a slight bow to both the ladies, raking the onlookers with his dark eyes. 'It seemed to me, my lady, that I caught something of a stale wind blowing over some old bones. Was there aught else that I should have heard?'

It was one of his own soldiers who stepped forward. A grey-headed Optio from his own Century. The man, whom Marcus knew to be a fighting soldier of great experience, would be the one to take charge if the Centurion was killed or gravely wounded, and was held in great respect by the rest of the troops.

'Yes, Publius?'

The man saluted, his face grave. 'Sir. Begging your pardon, sir, but these two ladies have been having something of a . . . a discussion, sir.'

'Go on.'

'Setting aside things that were said, that I would not care to have to repeat, this lady,' pointing to the wife of the merchant, 'claimed that she had a fighting man who was more than the equal of any of us.'

'And?'

'And, sir, I would like to cross swords with this Atilus she speaks of. I've seen him, sir, and he's a great fat hunk of grease. Very slow, sir. I'm sure I can take him easily, if you'll give me permission.'

Marcus fingered his lucky stone. To be caught fighting in a private matter was a grave offence against the military code. And if he condoned it, and the woman's slave was harmed, then there was no knowing where it might end. It was a tricky problem.

The Lady Agrippina solved it, in part, for him, coming close and taking him on one side. 'Have no worries about what will happen if your man slays her black. I will see that nothing happens to cause trouble. I will gladly pay any debts to settle for that underfed slut. Let them fight, Marcus, and you will not lack for a friend.'

'If I have the Lady Agrippina for a friend, then I will truly have little need of enemies,' said Marcus. But he said it only to himself.

'I thank you, my lady,' he said, bowing to her. 'I shall make the necessary arrangements for the combat as soon as possible. We must be back in Jerusalem within two days, or they will be sending out parties after us, fearing us taken by Zealots.'

'There's no arena here, sir,' interrupted the Optio. 'It'll have to be in the square.'

'And this black? This Atilus? What of him?'

Publius laughed. 'The day I can't beat a black like him, then that's the day I fall on my own sword. Truly, sir. He's along as a house-slave. All fat and no skill. It'll all be over before you can spit.'

So it was.

Before the fight began, Marcus made sure that everything was ready for their departure. Horses saddled and the carts loaded with the baggage of the Lady and the merchants. Agrippina herself sat under a shade, held for her by the same young boy who had been fanning her, while she sucked at another dish of sickly sweetmeats. Studiously ignoring, and ignored by, the diminutive wife of the merchant of vinegar.

The ring was made up by the soldiers, holding their javelins parallel to the ground to check any of the watching natives from breaking through, and to stop either of the men from breaking out.

Publius had taken off his armour and helmet, being content to fight in his tunic and leather kilt. It had been agreed that both men would fight with sword and dagger. As an experienced veteran, Publius kept his sword and dagger in excellent condition. Clean and polished in their scabbards, ornamented with red and yellow enamel. The shorter pugio also had its hilt bound with silver wire, and decorated with coloured glass.

There was no doubt in Marcus's mind that his man would be able to easily beat a cosseted house-slave. No doubt at all, until he saw the black.

Atilus Latrunculus. The Robber. Standing a half foot shorter than Marcus, which made him a little shorter than the Optio, yet weighing close to twice as much. He was one of the fattest men that Marcus had ever seen. The sword and pugio in his hands looked like the toys of a child. The soldiers burst into mocking laughter at his appearance, calling out at his grossness.

Marcus didn't laugh. His old trainer in warfare, Argos, had warned him against taking a first impression and acting on it. The puniest man might be an expert swordsman, and the fattest man could be a deadly opponent.

Marcus looked at the way Atilus moved. Saw that the fat wasn't the fat that eunuchs accumulated. Not the soft fat of easy living. There was a deal of muscle under that sweating black bulk.

The wife of the merchant clapped her bony hands together as Atilus came out, shuffling his feet in the hot sand, testing it. Moving the sword and dagger in his enormous hands.

'He's light on his feet, Publius. Take care with him. It may not be that easy.'

The Optio smiled at the young man's warning. 'Don't you worry, sir. My twelve year old daughter could beat him with a wooden sword.'

The thought brought back to Marcus a story that Argos had once told him. The one-eyed man had been a great gladiator in his day, and a mercenary soldier, hiring himself out to whoever would pay for his sword. It had been a warm autumn afternoon in the sand-dunes near the sea. A mile or so from their home among the flat marshes, at Gariannonum.

'Never take nothing for certain, Marcus,' he'd said. 'Reckon a man's dead when you've seen the blade split his heart. Not before. I had a mate years back. We were fighting against some tribe in the middle of Gaul. Beat them easy. After, we found this kid. Little girl. About twelve. Stone from a ballista we'd been using against their camp broke both her legs, and her arm. Right arm, it was. Poor little child. Weighed no more than a chicken. All skin and bone. Eyes sunk in with hunger. Torn dress on her.'

Marcus remembered he'd been fitting a new head to an old javelin as he talked. Slotting the tapered splice in the five-foot shaft, and easing in the two-foot iron shank. Hissing with concentration as he worked.

'This friend of mine felt sorry for her. It had been a devil of a battle. Most of her people were dead. Fires everywhere. She didn't cry as he picked her up. Didn't cry at all.'

Argos had paused at that point in his story, his eyes showing the pain of remembering the incident.

'But she had a thin dagger in her left hand, hidden up her sleeve. Only a bit longer than my middle finger. Thin, like a woman's bodkin. As he carried her, she nestled up against him, like any child would. And pushed her knife straight through his ear into his head. He fell like a stone down a well. Still, and unmoving. Didn't cry out. I was right behind him, and I nearly missed seeing it.'

A curlew had piped his thin song in the silence, and they could hear the waves mumbling on the distant beach. Marcus had asked him what had happened next.

'I saw he was dead. And I spotted the handle of the knife. The child fell as he dropped, and rolled away, spitting up at me like a demon from Hades. I looked down at her, seeing her broken limbs and poor wasted little body.' With a grunt he finally forced the blade of the spear home. 'And I set my foot to her neck and snapped it like a dry twig.'

The story of his old tutor, now long dead, came back to Marcus in that small square north of Jerusalem, as he watched Publius swaggering in front of his fellows, thinking that ponderous black would be an easy victim for him. And Marcus wondered if he had done right in letting them fight. But the Lady Agrippina, for all her faults, was right. No provincial woman, in her vulgar pride, could be allowed to mock the good name of the Roman Army.

It had to be.

The one thing that the soldier got right was that it would be a quick fight. As Marcus gave the signal for them to begin, Publius turned to his fellows, in a grin of bravado, then looked back and found that his death was upon him. Atilus had begun to move forward the moment the word was given, and his feet, surprisingly small in so vast a man, pattered across the sand in silence.

He reached Publius, and then dropped both of his weapons to the ground. As the soldier saw him, out of the corner of his eye, he cut at the black, but Atilus was quicker. Faster than anyone that Marcus had ever seen outside of the arena. And it was that thought that made him realize with a sick awareness that the wife of the merchant had tricked them.

Atilus might be their servant, but he was no ordinary servant. No house-boy, used to serving at the table or cleaning out the ovens. Marcus recognized him for what he was, and he cursed himself for not having seen it earlier. The black was a gladiator. A professional fighting machine.

Publius had no chance. A soldier might be reasonably useful with the tools of his trade. But he was no match for the needle-sharp training of the gladiator. Personal combat of this sort came rarely to a soldier, but a gladiator saw it and practised it every day of his life for hours on end.

The giant hunk of shimmering flesh brushed aside the sword, like a man would flick at a buzzing insect during a meal. Then ducked slightly, grabbed the right arm of the soldier, and broke it between his hands, grinding the splintered bones of the fore-arm together with a great grin of pleasure.

The woman clapped excitedly, screeching across to the white-faced Agrippina. 'I told you he was better. Your man is as good as dead. I shall not allow this tale to waste away with no telling.'

The happy anticipation among the rest of the troops of seeing Atilus cut to a bleeding mountain of fat had vanished as though it had never been. There had been some rowdy cheers at the beginning, before Marcus had given the signal to start. The victory had been so overwhelming and so total, that there was complete silence in the square, as they waited for the final stroke to be made.

Publius had stepped away, face as white as bone, with beads of sweat dripping to the sand. The sword lay near his feet, and Atilus motioned to him to pick it up, smiling broadly at the Optio's distress.

'Don't!' shouted Marcus. 'Stand off him and try and cut his hands if he comes in!'

It was the best advice he could think of. But crippled as he was, despite the fact that the black had no weapon at all, Publius couldn't follow it. As Atilus came in at him, hands outstretched, fingers flexing like thick snakes, the soldier lost his nerve. Publius could have stood shoulder to shoulder with a line of comrades in a stricken field, and never wavered. Had done, on more than one occasion. Or faced a charge of cavalry, or chariots driven by naked screaming savages and scarcely blinked.

But this was different. Alone, and with the pain from the

savagely broken arm almost making him faint, with his doom stalking up on him, teeth bared, his nerve went and he turned to run, the dagger still gripped, forgotten, in his left hand.

Effortlessly, without seeming to hurry, Atilus went after him. It was in some way obscene that such a hugely fat man should be able to move so swiftly over the shifting sand of the town square, catching up the soldier before he'd gone ten paces. An arm reached out and grabbed him by the back of the neck, pulling him into a smothering embrace. At thc last, Publius made a valiant effort to stab the black, straining his arm round behind his back, but Atilus merely laughed. The first noise he'd made at all, and it was a disgusting sound. A thin, bubbling noise, like air being forced through honey.

He was still tittering as he crushed the other arm to a mangled, dangling useless hank of flesh, hugging the Roman to him, gradually lifting him off the ground, until his legs flailed and kicked at the air. Atilus slowly turned to face his mistress, little eyes buried in rolls of fat, waiting for her to signal.

'To the death, I think we agreed, my dear Agrippina, did we not?' she asked, smiling through her thin lips at the angry face of the lady at her side.

Agrippina made no reply, and the merchant's wife merely turned back to face her champion, and nodded once to him. He bared his teeth in answer, and heaved Publius up, holding him clean above his head. The soldier was no small man, and it was a very considerable feat of strength to hold him like that. One hand gripping him by the neck, the other clasping his thigh in so tight a grip that the flesh bulged between Atilus's fingers.

'Let me stick the bastard!' called out one of the soldiers in the ring, furious that they'd been tricked so easily. Publius had been popular, and could have hoped to make Centurion in the next year or so.

'No!' snapped Marcus, clasping his hand so hard round the pommel of his sword that his knuckles showed white under the strain. 'There was a wager and all agreed to it. There is naught to do.'

Very slowly, his eyes now fixed immovably on Marcus, the giant lowered the struggling figure until its back rested across his thighs. Then he knelt down, holding Publius over his knee, back arched like a drawn bow, and waited. Marcus knew exactly what Atilus planned to do, and knew that there was no power on earth could save anyone held like that. The Optio had been one of the men allotted to him, as their officer, and now he was going to die. That pushed him to a decision.

'When you have done with that man, I will show you a trick or two,' he called out.

At first Atilus took no notice, and Marcus wondered if he knew any Latin. 'I will show you something, if your heart is not as weak as your body is fat. Or are you too frightened to face a man who knows the ways of the arena?'

The charge of cowardice reached the fat man, and he smiled. With a decisive thrust downwards, he broke the spine of Publius over his knee, as a man might strive to crack a bundle of kindling, and stood up, heaving the corpse over the side of the square, where it landed with a wet thump at Marcus's feet. There was little sign of Publius's suffering now he was dead. His eyes were open, and his jaw gaped, with a little blood, where he must have bitten either his tongue or his lips in his death-throes. One arm was folded under him, and the other flapped across the dirt at an unnatural angle.

'There is your great soldier. Now I will kill you too, if you do not run away and mess yourself with fright. But I will kill you slowly.'

Feeling his heart pounding with the thought of what he had just committed himself to, Marcus walked slowly over to where Agrippina had risen to her feet at his words. He waved a hand to shut up the chattering of his men, talking furiously among themselves at the words of their young officer.

'Lady. It was all a trick. That man is a gladiator. I know this for certain. That woman tricked you, and has made you look a fool. And has made the Army of Rome look fools. And has made me, an officer of the army, look foolish. There is a way that we can strike back at her.'

All this was delivered in a quiet whisper, his lips almost touching the ear of the older woman. She looked up at him, and he was surprised to see that her eyes were wet with tears.

'Marcus Britannicus. I had not thought that the . . . that the soldier would die. Never.'

He glanced across at where the black had squatted in the dust at the feet of his mistress, while she patted him on the head and kneaded the ridges of fat and muscle at the back of his neck.

'That man, that Atilus, is one of the best gladiators that I have ever seen in my life. Short though that life may be, I have yet seen all of the best. His worth can scarcely be calculated to that merchant. He is almost priceless. Yet, I do think that he can be beaten.'

'No. Marcus, I cannot allow you to try. If a soldier of the valour of that poor man could do nothing, then what chance would a beardless youth like you have?'

'Publius died because he never thought that such a gross man could be a fighter. He was wrong, and he died. Atilus will think me a foolish boy, angry at one of my men being slain, and blinded by that anger to the reality of dying. He will never think that a young boy might yet have the skill to defeat him. And he will die.'

There was a long pause. Marcus could hear his men still talking, doubtless thinking him mad to challenge such a killing machine. Yet he truly believed that he might win. The training of Argos had been long and painful and very, very thorough. He felt sure that Atilus was there to be taken. That the first impression of professional skill was false, and that time would prove who was the better.

Agrippina looked up at him, and her hand rose to touch his face. 'I wish you well, Marcus Britannicus. If you die, you can die in the knowledge that I will carry the manner of your passing to my grave with me, and that never will I hear a word against your father.'

'And if I live, my lady. What then?'

'Then you will have a friend who will stand beside you for ever. And I will talk to my husband, and you may find him not without influence. Should the military life not be for you, then there will be other things that you can do.' She shook her head. 'No. This is madness, boy. That giant will devour you and there will not be even the bones left for us to scavenge and bury. It cannot be.'

'I have challenged him. Would you have a further shame added to the name of Rome? That we fight and lose is bad enough. But to lose without fighting. That is worse.'

There was no argument. She nodded her reluctant approval,

and went back to her seat, brushing the slave boy aside. It was obvious to Marcus that she had little faith in his ability to win the fight, and having seen Atilus in action, he had to admit she had every reason for feeling doubt. Whatever doubts he may have had about her were removed by her actions as she sat down.

Eyes up, staring straight at the wife of the merchant, Agrippina said: 'Madam. Your gladiator has tricked a valiant soldier of Rome to his death. I doubt that you will ever know the meaning of the word "shame", but I hope to make you remember your error for all your days.'

There was a shrill laugh from the woman, and the revolting bubbling giggle from the black at her words. 'So, my lady. You now think your beardless champion there will settle with Atilus?'

Marcus knew that she didn't think that, but he almost loved her for her next words. 'I do not think it. I *know* it. And I will prove my faith in him with money, unless you are frightened to wager.'

Just for a split fraction of a moment, Marcus saw doubt in the eyes of the big gladiator, and he knew that Atilus truly could be killed. Despite his size and strength and skill, the fat man lacked the cold edge of confidence. But his mistress had no such doubts.

Her head went back, and she brayed her amusement like an Ostia fishwife. Which, perhaps, she might once have been. 'You wish to risk your money as well. My dear Agrippina, I could hardly do that. The lives of soldiers are one thing, of very little worth. But gold and silver.'

'One hundred aurei that Marcus Britannicus defeats your man. And kills him.'

'One hundred aurei!'

'I said that. One hundred aurei. And that is what I mean. Is it too much for you to hazard?'

The soldiers had fallen quiet, but the size of the bet brought a burst of chattering, that only stopped when Marcus shouted at them.

'No. No, of course not.' Marcus grinned to himself. The woman betrayed her feelings in a way that most high-bred ladies of Rome would have found laughable. It was clear that the wager – an enormous sum of money – was far more than she had expected, but she dared not back out now.

'Then we are agreed. To the death, and with one hundred aurei on the outcome.'

'I would not concern myself even if the wager were to be double that.'

Agrippina smiled at her, casting a sideways glance at Marcus. 'Double. Done, my dear. Two hundred aurei it is.'

'But . . .'

'Of course. It *is* too much, isn't it, for someone like you who only a few months ago had hardly two denarii to rub together. Let us forget it and . . .'

'No.' The voice was a strangled gasp, and Marcus thought for a moment that the woman would have a fit. Veins stood out in her stringy neck, and she half-rose, looking to Atilus for support.

'Well? What is the wager, madam? Let us have it clear so that all may witness it.'

'Two hundred. Yes, two hundred that Atilus kills that young cockerel. You can do it, can you not, Atilus?'

There it was again. The note of doubt. Doubt that a lady of the eminence of Agrippina Germanicus would risk such a sum unless she had great confidence in her man. And Atilus was picking up the sword and pugio, balancing them in his soft hands. This time he would not be taking the risk of casting them aside. This time he would be more careful. Yet there would still be that contempt for this fool who insisted on throwing away his life.

Once he had stripped off ready, in the same way that poor Publius had, Marcus marched to where Agrippina sat, and leaned over her. 'Madam. That is a great wager. I trust that I shall prove worthy of it.'

'If you don't,' she said, through a mouthful of honey and nuts, 'then it will be no great loss to me. It is worth the wager simply to see the shock on that slut's face.'

He stood up, when she pulled him down again, her fingers sticky on his smooth skin. 'But that is not all the reason, my little Marcus. There is something in you. I am not a fool, and I think that I am a judge of a man. I think that you can beat him. With that wager sitting on his fat shoulders, it might just distract his mind for a moment.' And she smiled at him.

'My lady. I will be in your debt if I beat Atilus. I would be happy if there was to be some way that I could repay you for your trust.'

His words were deliberately ambiguous, and he saw a hint of a blush on her sun-reddened cheeks.

'I think, Marcus Britannicus,' she whispered, her voice hardly reaching his ears, 'that I might just be able to think of some way that you could serve me.'

He straightened up, saluting her, bringing his arm across his body with military efficiency. 'Lady Agrippina. You have given me all the courage I need and the reason to slay that gross black dog.'

Atilus heard him, as he was supposed to do, and snarled at him across the makeshift arena, in his high, girl's voice: 'You will die hard, Roman. I will promise you that by all the Gods.'

'And I swear by Jupiter Optimus Maximus that it will be you who die.' Privately he pattered a prayer to his own deity. The old god: Mithras.

The sword felt light in his hand, balanced by the shorter dagger. He flexed his shoulder muscles, feeling the sun strike hot on his bare flesh. He had chosen to fight without sandals, preferring the sand under his toes. He looked across at Atilus, wondering for a moment if he was about to commit suicide in a particularly nasty way.

Marcus was something of a fatalist, and the bad times that he'd been through after the death of his father had made him place a low value on life. If he was going to die now – today – then that must be what Mithras intended for him, and he couldn't do anything about it. But if he was going to be killed, he was damned if he was going to go meekly, with a lowered head, like an ox before the stunning hammer of the slaughterer. He would fight.

'Fight!' cried out the soldier in charge of the combat. One of the patrol, chosen by Marcus for his steadiness. He was not the sort of man who would lose his nerve and try and kill the black. He had been given an order by Marcus, and he would obey it, even if it meant standing by unmoving while his young officer was butchered.

At the word, Atilus came floating towards him, arms stretched out wide, a huge grin on his face. Licking his blubbery red lips, and whistling softly to himself. Marcus moved away, careful, balanced on the balls of his feet. Ready for a sudden rush.

'Come, boy. Lay down your weapons and kneel before me, and I may even spare you. At best I'll kill you quickly.'

Marcus ignored him. Argos had warned him against the men who talked. They were dangerous. They would try and lure you off your guard with their words. He was conscious of the merchant's wife sitting watching, a hungry expression on her thin face. In the tension of the moment, Marcus noticed that a pulse beat in the woman's forehead, over her right eye. Alongside her, almost close enough to touch, sat Agrippina, a strained look on her face. She saw him glance at her, and flashed him a quick, nervous smile.

'Stop your dancing, boy, or you'll make me angry, and then I'll make it slow. Very slow.'

It was damnably hot in the square. Sweat rivered across the fat man's rolls of stomach, dripping silently to the sand. There was just the barest suggestion of panting in his breath, and Marcus smiled and moved further and faster, luring him on. It may be that the black was immensely strong and quick, but it also seemed that he was sadly out of condition.

'Will you stand and fight?' he snarled, stopping still, and rubbing his eyes with the back of his hand.

'Your boy is a coward, my lady,' snapped the wife of the merchant.

'I fear that your husband's cheap vinegar has soured your tongue, madam,' answered Marcus, who happened to be near her at that moment.

There was no reply, but Atilus had seen the lapse as he turned away, and came in, sword thrusting, and the dagger drawn back ready for the second cut. Marcus whirled about, parrying the sword easily with his own blade, slicing with his dagger at the fat man's outstretched arm.

Cutting him, just inside the elbow, bloodying his knife. For a moment, he couldn't tell how serious the wound was going to be. In a pass as swift as that it was impossible to judge how deep the blade had gone in. Whether it was just a skin cut, or whether there was damage to the muscles or the tendons. His first thought was that it had been deep, but he hadn't allowed for the gross fatness of the man, buffering the arm from serious damage.

Cursing and spitting like a scalded kitchen slave, Atilus backed away, looking down at his arm, wiping away the blood, glaring at his opponent. There was a burst of cheering from the soldiers, and he heard a woman's voice, raised in encouragement.

'First blooding!' called out the soldier who was acting as the judge of the contest. 'First blood to Marcus Julius Britannicus!'

Next time, Atilus would be more careful.

He came shuffling in, the grin gone from his face, the two blades weaving and dancing, the harsh light of the afternoon sun bouncing off them. Marcus kept his distance, making sure that the black never managed to get him cornered. Trapped in a position where his greater strength and weight would be an overwhelming advantage.

The calling and cheering died away from the soldiers, as the fight dropped back into its pattern of move and follow. It was a pattern that worked to Marcus's advantage and he knew that Atilus wouldn't allow him to keep it going for very much longer.

Marcus made a forward move, and the fat man backed away from him, almost running, until he seemed to catch his feet against a stone and fell backwards.

He knew that the inexperienced youth would come running in to strike at him while he lay helpless. Letting go of the dagger, he scratched up a handful of the dry sand, and hurled it at where he knew his enemy's face would be.

It wasn't.

Marcus had known about that trick by the time he was ten years old, and he'd been ready for it. It was true what he'd said about the gladiator to Agrippina. Because he found it impossible to take such a young opponent seriously, he somehow thought that Marcus would be easier to fool. As soon as the big man stumbled clumsily backwards, Marcus had been ready for the trick with the dirt.

By the time it came, and the cloud of choking sand was thrown at him, he'd moved to one side, sword transferred to his left hand, and the knife held by its needle point in his right. Argos had made sure that he could fight and throw with both hands. But he favoured his natural right hand, and his tutor had drilled into him to take any advantage that was offered.

Atilus grinned through the dust, half rising, sword reaching out eagerly for the flesh of the boy. The boy who wasn't there. The smile vanished with the sand, and he saw Marcus, standing easily, poised to throw the knife.

It would have been simple for Marcus to have sent the blade speeding through the layers of fat to seek out the pounding heart, and still it for ever with one thunder blow. That would have been easy for him, and easy too for Atilus. And he didn't wish the black to have an easy passing to whatever gods he worshipped.

The knife thudded into Atilus's right shoulder, tearing into the joint, bringing a high, thin scream of pain from the man, like a gelded stallion. The sword dropped to the sand, and he tried to make a recovery with his left hand. He was good. Very good. There was always a temptation in a fight to stand off when some trick or other had worked, and give yourself a clap on the back for your skill. While you were doing that a more skilled fighter would have spilled your tripes in the mud.

Ignoring the wound, after that single shocked cry, Atilus went for the knife with his left hand, picking it up, ready to defend himself. And again he was just that moment too slow.

Marcus was in on him, the sword still in his left hand, cutting at the rising knife, striking cleanly through the chubby wrist, so that the hand was severed and fell in the red sand, the fingers still clutching the hilt of the pugio, until they slowly relaxed. Blood jetted in a bright fountain, high in the air, from the stump of the arm, splattering in Marcus's face, almost blinding him.

With one hand he wiped away the hot saltiness, stepping back like a craftsman admiring his handiwork. Now there was no danger to him. Atilus was dead. Still standing, trying to check the flow of blood, but a dead man. Strangely, there was no cheering from the soldiers, as they waited for the final stroke that would end it.

And again, Marcus withheld it. He intended that Atilus should suffer. Carefully, holding the sword out at arm's length,

Marcus moved closer. Crippled though Atilus was, he still took care. But the man was weeping, great tears trickling down his fat face.

'Please, spare me, master. Let me have help for my arm. I beg you.'

Marcus spat in the spreading pool of blood by the man's feet. 'Spare you! You and your mistress still have a little of your lesson to learn. That Rome is not to be joked about by filth like you. That good soldiers aren't to be murdered to give pleasure to petty natives!'

'Please. I'm bleeding to death.'

'There's plenty of blood left in you. Atilus, you're just a great tub. A great stinking tub of noisome stench. An offence to the eyes and minds of honest citizens. And you will soon be gone, and the earth a little cleaner for it.'

'Watch for the flood from the tub, sir!' called out one of the soldiers, raising a bellow of laughter from the rest.

The sun was beginning to sink behind the mountains to the east, and Marcus wanted to be moving and safely in camp miles away before dark. It was time to finish it.

Quick as an adder's tongue, the blade flicked out at the helpless black, and each time there was a new stream of blood to melt into the river from the severed arm. A cut on the chest, across one drooping breast. The other on the face. Opening the corner of Atilus's mouth in a hideous leer, baring the white of teeth through the cut until they were drowned in blood.

'Again!' shouted one of the troops, and Agrippina was also on her feet, hands clutching a torn rag of linen that she had been holding during the fight.

Atilus staggered back, his hand going up to his mouth, smearing blood over his chin and neck. Again Marcus slashed at him, this time taking off an ear. The black's hand went up so fast to feel the new wound that some of the soldiers didn't see it, and Marcus could hear them asking each other what had happened.

'The ear. The tub's ear. Ripped off.'

'Serve him right,' called out Agrippina, unable to hide her feelings behind the mask of self-control required of a Roman lady.

It was no sort of fight. It was simple butchery, with Marcus using his greater speed and mobility to move in, strike with either sword or pugio, retrieved from the sand, and then slip away from the dying man with the ease and silence of a midwinter ghost.

The gladiator's body streamed with blood from a dozen cuts, and Marcus was amazed that he still stood. Finally tiring of the exercise, he feinted again at Atilus's face, causing the black to try and lift his arm to defend himself. Then he thrust under the raised hand, feeling the blade grate between ribs, before he buried it in the man's massive carcass. There was a deep groan, and the body slumped to the dirt of the town square, the life ebbing away from it. As Marcus pushed with his foot against the inert flesh to draw out the sword, it was as if the living force had fled, and he stood over a heap of mangled meat.

There was a great cheer from his soldiers at his victory, and Agrippina rushed to him, and threw her arms about him, so that he could feel her breasts pressing against his sweating chest.

'Marcus Britannicus! You were simply wonderful. Wait till my dear husband hears of this. He will want to meet you.'

'Thank you lady,' he said quietly. 'Now there might be time for that service that we promised each other. It will take two days to get to Jerusalem.'

'Two days?'

'And two nights.'

She squeezed his hand, feeling it slick with wet blood and perspiration. Then she turned to face the wife of the merchant, who had walked unsteadily to stand over the carcass of her champion, and gazed down at it with an expression of horror and disbelief. As though she had seen a mouse strike down a mighty pine-tree. Her face was very pale, and her mouth worked with the tension.

'Madam!' Agrippina had to repeat the call twice more before her words penetrated. 'There is a debt between us, is there not?'

'What?' The voice was scarcely audible, almost drowned by the wind that always sprang up in the desert as the day wore towards its end.

'A debt. Two hundred aurei, I think, was the amount. Was it not?'

'Yes. Yes, it was. But . . .'

'But what?'

'Atilus. How can I tell him that Atilus is dead, and that I . . .? He paid near four hundred for him to a trader and thought that he would take him to Jerusalem and make our fortunes. Now he's dead, *and* I've lost all that gold as well. Oh!'

And she fell to her knees and was sick all over the sand, the vomit mingling with the blood of her gladiator. Agrippina smiled at the sight, and turned to Marcus.

'She will not do that again, I think, my young hero. Not again.'

Marcus nodded, already preoccupied with the problems of getting the men and the travellers on the move. He looked down at the giant corpse. 'He was a great fighter, my lady.'

'Yet you cut him to pieces, and denied him a quick passing.'

He shook his head, walking slowly away from the trampled, bloody sand of the square. 'If he had fought like a man, then he would not have died like a dog.'

The sun was setting.

FOUR

'Again, my brave young warrior. We will be at Jerusalem, and it will not be easy to slip away from my husband in a camp. Again.'

'To hear is to obey, my lady,' he muttered, rolling over towards Agrippina, his hand groping for her heavy breasts. She loved him to spend time over her breasts, massaging and caressing them. Licking the nipples, and taking them between his lips, nipping them gently with his sharp teeth, until she moaned and clung to him, her hand going down, over his flat stomach, finding his maleness, encircling it, the rough-cut rings on her fingers scraping at his erection, making him wince.

She felt him jerk, and pulled back, her big eyes looking across the tent at him. 'What's wrong, Marcus? Have you no love left for me?'

'Agrippina. I have love and more to spare, as I have tried to show you over the last two days.'

'And right well have you shown it to me. I gave you my word that I should not forget you. You may always look to myself and to Flavius Germanicus for friendship. When I tell him of the fight, he will want to meet you.'

That wasn't quite what Marcus wanted. When they got back to Jerusalem, the only thing he wished was to get out to this rock of Masada and kill Zealots. It was well enough to lie with a woman of the rank and worldliness of Agrippina, but it was quite another to calmly clasp the hand of her husband in friendship, knowing what he had done.

'Remember that I will urge him to gift you with fifty of the aurei.'

Marcus hadn't forgotten that. The wife of the merchant had agreed to pay the debt when they reached the city, not having anywhere near that sort of gold about her. For the whole journey she had remained in her wagon, with her maidservant, and nothing had been seen of her. She had even refused to come out to eat.

It wasn't just the rings that had made Marcus sore. The lady was an insatiable lover, and had insisted that they should spend as much time as possible together on the journey, pressing him to eat with her, so that she might tear down his under-garments and feast on his muscular body draining him with a lust that he had never encountered before.

He privately thanked Mithras that they were nearly at Jerusalem. He'd heard of the women in Rome who kept their oiled and perfumed lovers, like apes on a chain, to entertain them when they wished it. He'd also heard of what happened to these kept men when their wealthy mistresses tired of them, or when they became an embarrassment to them with their demands for new jewels. Or when their husbands began to suspect that there might be something in the whispering of the clacking tongues.

There had been a time in the arena at Rome, when near every person there, from senator to slave knew what was happening. The only man who didn't know was the husband of the lady concerned. She had a lover, who had begun to think himself a creature of some importance to her. And she had decided it was time for a change.

The wretch had been muted with the hot irons, and stripped naked, and wrapped in the hide of a female ox, so that the sexual organs of the dead beast were about his own loins. Spread-eagled, his head protruding so that the crowd could enjoy his suffering, he was brought out into the centre of the ampitheatre, and tied there tightly.

While his mistress lay back in her box, and caressed her cuckold husband, her lover sweated in the heat of the arena, able to see her, and unable to cry out. And she continued to watch him, when they brought in the bulls, and encouraged them to mount the man, tearing him apart in agony.

And she had laughed as he died.

It had been scant consolation to the dead man when her carriage had overturned on the way home that evening, and both she and her husband had died in the tangled wreckage.

Marcus didn't intend to die in the arena. Not like that anyway. Bound and helpless. For the first time, though, at the urging of Agrippina, he found himself wondering whether the solution to many of his problems might not come in the games. He had killed Atilus, who would have been considered a worthy opponent in any amphitheatre anywhere. And he'd had the best of training from Argos. There was money in being a top gladiator. As a freeborn Roman citizen, there was only one risk for him. That he might die.

After the death of his father, money had been in short supply. And here was a door that was swinging open in front of him, with the lady promising that her husband would sponsor him in training, and would look after him as his protector.

He stored the thought away, and turned his attention again to the needs of the lady. And, if the truth were told, he didn't find it a chore without enjoyment. And she seemed to find pleasure in it.

As his father used to say: 'You catch more flies with honey than you do with vinegar.'

The morning of the last day they were nearing Jerusalem, their dust cloud rising into a clear blue sky, the horizon bounded by great orange hunks of mountains, towering upwards with jagged tips. There were a dozen men in the patrol, with three wagons, and a carriage for the Lady Agrippina. Marcus rode at the head of the column on his favourite stallion, the big black, called Pluto, after the implacable God of the Underworld. He had been a gift from his father, in the last of the good years, before the scandalmongers ended the happiness. A mighty, red-eyed beast, he was near unrideable to any man but Marcus.

Pluto was skittish, swishing his tail angrily at the multitude of flies that swarmed about the column. Marcus sat him easily, holding him on a tight rein, knowing from past painful experience what happened when he gave the animal his head.

The trail was narrow, passing through a ravine, with sheer walls, dropping to slopes of scree and tumbled boulders. It was, he thought, a fine place for an ambush if the Zealots were so minded.

'Good place for a trap, sir.'

The words were so close to his own thoughts that Marcus

jumped, turning in the saddle to see the smiling face of the soldier who'd held the square for him during the fight against Atilus. His name was Decius, and he'd been with the Tenth for nearly fifteen years. When they got back, there'd be a place for an Optio, and they both knew that Marcus was likely to recommend him for the post. Apart from the extra power, there was also the extra money. And Decius had a wife and eight children back in Rome.

'Yes, it is. But they say the Jews are stuck up at their tower.'

'Masada.'

'You've been there?'

Decius nodded, pushing back his helmet to wipe the salt sweat from his head. Despite the padding round the rim of the helmet, it had still chafed a ring of raw flesh from his forehead, as it had with every man of the Legion. It was almost like a slave ring.

'Great heap! Like a mountain of stinking shit, stuck in the middle of nowhere, with one way up and one way down. And the Jews at every corner. I don't envy our Flavius, trying to take it. He'll get there in the end, even if he has us tearing the hill down with our bare hands and carting it away in little bits. They won't win.'

For a few more minutes they rode along in silence, their horses' hooves clinking on the stone. The men behind were also silent, their usual good humour drowned in the heat and the oppressive feeling of the surrounding rocks. The curtains on the Lady Agrippina Germanicus's carriage were drawn. At the rear of the column, the wife of the vinegar merchant stuck her head out to ask how much further.

'She'll get a hot reception from her man, when he gets his hands on her, sir. After what you did to his gladiator, and after what old Big. . . Beg pardon, sir. After what the lady took off her by way of gold. Can't wait to see them get together in the city.'

'Will you be coming to Masada with me, Decius?'

Marcus liked the soldier, and admired his knowledge of fighting. He had instinctively felt that the narrow valley would be a fine place for an ambush.

'Like to, sir. But I'd fancy a chance to get back to Rome and see the wife and the children again, if that . . .'

The spear took him through his open mouth, smashing

through teeth, breaking his jaw, and burying its point in the lower part of his brain. Decius rolled backwards out of the high saddle, crashing among the stones at the side of the road. His horse reared, neighing in terror at the sudden smell of blood, galloping away down the ravine, its hooves striking sparks from the pebbles.

The spear was followed by more, hissing through the air with the unmistakable sound of death. Marcus leaned forward over Pluto's neck, drawing his sword, looking for the numbers of their attackers, and where they were hiding. There were arrows humming as well, and cries from further back told of casualties.

'Dismount, and fight on foot!!' he yelled, swinging out of the saddle, trying to keep his horse between himself and the ambushing Jews. It had to be the Jews. There were no other enemies of Rome so near to Jerusalem that would dare to attack an armed party of troops. It must be Zealots, perhaps mistaking the column for a money train, or supplies for the camp in the city.

'Form round me! Come on, lads. To me! Out of the wagons, all of you!!'

There was still no sign of their attackers. Just the steady rain of missiles from behind cover, rattling among them, and occasionally picking at a man or a mount. Marcus quickly counted what was left.

Nine men, including himself. Lady Agrippina, muttering to herself about the damned Jews, squatting in the dust, behind Marcus, her gown tucked up round her knees. There were a half dozen slaves, one of them moaning to herself, with an arrow sticking out of her shoulder, that nobody had time to pull out for her. And there was the wife of the vinegar merchant, pulling one of her slaves from behind a dead horse so that she could shelter there herself.

With all of his senior troops dead, Marcus had nobody to ask for ideas. He was on his own, pinned down by what must be a superior force, with no way out. All he could do was sit there and wait for them to show themselves. And maybe he could persuade them to do that a bit sooner, before his command was cut quite to pieces.

Spent arrows pattered in the road about them, and Marcus

called for his men to gather up a few, then told them his plan. Within moments, one of his men stood up, shouted out, then fell back clutching at a shaft in his chest. Followed by another. And a third, all holding the arrows that had hit them.

Agrippina whispered to him, as though she might be overheard. 'May I help? I can pretend a death as well as any man.'

Marcus nodded. It would help to make it look more real if one of the ladies faked dying. With a convincing scream, she held an arrow pressed to her capacious bosom and toppled back in a welter of blowing skirts and firm thighs.

There was a harsh cry from up on the top of the hill, and the shooting stopped. It was only with a quick word that Marcus was able to stop one of the young soldiers from going ahead with their plan and pretending to have been shot by an arrow that wasn't being fired.

For a moment there was an uneasy brooding silence, broken by one of the Roman horses, wounded with three arrows, one in its nostrils, scrambling to its feet and making off at a crooked gallop down the ravine towards Jerusalem. Again there was the harsh cry, and a flight of arrows went hissing after the beast, some of which must have hit it. But its gait continued seemingly unaffected, and it was soon out of sight, though they could hear its hooves for some time.

Marcus lay flat on the ground, holding his sword in his right hand, dagger ready in his left. His helmet felt uncomfortable, and he quietly took it off, and laid it among the pebbles. The sun was high overhead, baking the ground to blazing heat. Flies buzzed from nowhere, attracted by the blood that congealed in the dust. One of the women, the wounded slave he thought, was still weeping, moaning to herself in a foreign tongue that Marcus didn't recognize.

Then, there was the noise of horses. About a dozen, he guessed, coming towards them from the way they'd come. It must be the rest of the ambushers, closing the door on them in case they'd tried to make a run for it back down the road. They were trotting nearer, then there was a shout, and the trot became a gallop, accompanied by cries and cheers.

'Ready!' called Marcus, loud enough for his men to hear. 'Here they come!'

It was hard to wait, there on the earth, knowing that light

cavalry was charging down on you; screaming enemies, whose sole purpose was to kill you or to make you a prisoner so that their women could work their obscenities on your helpless bodies. He risked a glance round the rump of Pluto, who crouched quivering, ready to bolt at a moment.

The road was narrow and wound among the cliffs, making it hard to see far. A cloud of dust seemed to be winding towards them, and it was from the heart of the cloud that the wild cries came.

'All right, lads. At my word. Take them when they least expect it. Hold still and wait. Don't move. If any of you go and get killed before I tell you to, then I'll see him on Centurion's report in the morning.'

It wasn't a great jest, but it raised a ripple of laughter at a moment when it would have been easier to have run screaming from the attackers.

The clatter of the hooves swelled to a beat of thunder, the cries and yells sounding like fiends from Hades. Another glance to judge the moment.

'Now!!' he screamed, his voice cracking with the tension and excitement.

He was the first out from cover, finding one of the horsemen right on top of him, a spear couched under his arm, pointing at him. Precious though horses were, it never for a moment entered Marcus's mind to try and spare the beast. As it rose over him, rearing up, whinnying at his sudden appearance from under its hooves, he cut at its forelegs. One slash with the sword, and one with the knife. Crippling it, then dodging as it screamed its pain, and rolled over, crushing its rider under it. Trapping him by one leg.

The whole area was a whirlpool of dust as the Romans came to life, stabbing and cutting like madmen, bringing down horses and riders in a dance of bloody death. The other Jews, hidden among the rocks, were useless, blinded by the sand, and unable to risk a shot with either bow or spear, for fear of bringing down their own men. Marcus based his strategy on the fact that they would hesitate, none of them wishing to break cover. Waiting for an order. And their leader might also wait. Trying to see what was happening, not wanting to commit the rest of his force if it wasn't necessary.

Pausing only to snuff out the life of the rider under the fallen horse, running his sword through the struggling man's throat, Marcus whirled into the centre of the fray. A sword flashed at his face, and he parried, slipping his pugio into the Jew's ribs. The battle degenerated into a shambles, with the Romans having the immense advantage of their armour and their military discipline. Four of them had grouped together, cutting a swath of blood through the unseated Zealots, and Marcus joined them, hacking their way about, until it seemed as though there were scarcely any left.

As the trampling of the horses stopped, with them all either down or fled, so the picture cleared. There were still six of the Romans up, though two of them had wounds that sprayed blood over their armour, to run dark over their bare legs to the dirt. The women and the slaves still all looked as though they were all right. One of the Jews who'd been unhorsed, and who had a jagged edge of broken bone sticking through the flesh of his thigh, was crawling towards them.

The wife of the merchant covered up her face, screaming at the top of her voice. Agrippina simply looked across to where Marcus and the rest stood watching.

'Move out of the . . .' Marcus's words were strangled in his throat, as he saw the rest of the Zealots suddenly come from cover further down the ravine, all mounted. Though they'd broken the back of the first attack, with not a Zealot alive and on his feet, there were now another dozen, or more, thundering towards them. Barely five hundred feet away, surrounded by a wraith of dust, pillaring up to the sky. They wouldn't be caught by the same trick now.

Marcus had seen enough of warfare to know that they had two chances. Very small. And none at all. He dragged his men in closer, so they presented a solid block. One that the horses, unless they were trained as fighting cavalry mounts, might swing away from. And he threw his dagger to Agrippina, so that it stuck in the soft soil only inches from her hand. With a quick smile she took it, and waited for the injured Zealot to reach her.

Then the horsemen were on them, and the curtain of trampled sand blotted out everything. For a moment, Marcus's memory went back to Britain, and the dreaded light cavalry of his great-aunt, Boadicea. Small men, in light basket-work chariots, drawn by pairs of ponies. And others, also on the sturdy ponies, sniping at the flanks of the enemy forces. He'd been a lad of just five summers when the Iceni had revolted, rising against the Romans, and beating them in several engagements.

There was a vivid vision in his mind's eye of the tall Queen, with her bright red hair flaming like a banner of rebellion, leading her men. And he remembered his mother's tears at the humiliation and whipping that had followed their ultimate full-scale revolt. And then the day that the messenger brought news of the battle against Paulinus and the Fourteenth and Twentieth Legions. And how his aunt had been found among the heap of human and animal corpses that was all the Romans left in their anger. They said she had poisoned herself.

The Twentieth had among their Legates one Lucian Julius that day. Marcus's father. His mother, Elfleda, had never truly recovered.

And now his own life was going to end here, in a rocky defile, almost within spitting distance of Jerusalem, at the hands of a few Jewish Zealots.

Two. Then three of his comrades fell in the mêlée, ridden down by the superior numbers of the enemy. They swirled about him, blinding him, so that he could hardly see who or what he cut at. Faces moved by, and cloaks billowed in the movement. Eyes, mouths, open, shouting in a language he couldn't understand. Swords cutting at him. Blood splattering warm in his face, and Marcus not even knowing whether it came from himself. From a friend. Or from an enemy, or even an enemy's mount. Time after time he felt his sword grate against bone, or slice through flesh. Men screamed, and once a falling body nearly toppled him to the sand.

Another Roman went down, sliding forward like a swimmer entering deep water, the sword falling from his hand. Marcus began to pray to Mithras. Quietly at first, then louder, as he felt the pangs of fatigue wearing him down, and saw the end coming closer.

'Hold, the Tenth!!!'

Marcus had heard poets tell of how men at the point of death heard their rescue coming and thought only that it was a dream.

He didn't. No dream shouted out like that, in the bull's roar of a Centurion of the Legion.

'To me, the Tenth!' he called back, feeling his voice dry and strained. 'To me, the Tenth!!'

The other two living Romans took up the cry, and heard it returned twenty-fold. The area around them cleared as though by magic, and Marcus could see again. He swept the pass with his eyes, taking in what was happening at one glance.

The Jews were fleeing, riding like the wind away from the city, two of them slumped over their saddles, nearly toppling off, showing that the Romans had sold their lives dearly. And coming down the pass the other way, from the direction of Jerusalem, riding in a tight formation, cutting like a wedge through the handful of Zealots who'd tried to escape that way, came a cohort of the Tenth. Armour gleaming and helmets twinkling in the sun.

The sand was strewn with the corpses of animals and people. The huddled group of slaves lived, hiding behind the one wagon still upright.

Agrippina?

She sat astride the body of the Jew with the broken leg, her knees digging into his shoulders. The man's arms still moved feebly, showing he was alive. But Agrippina was sawing industriously at the back of his neck with Marcus's knife, blood streaked up her arms like a kitchen slave butchering a goose.

Spitting dust, Marcus grinned and waved a hand to the Centurion on his white horse as they swept towards them. The wife of the vinegar merchant also stood up, tears streaming over her thin cheeks with the relief of having survived.

At that moment, almost under the hooves of the leading cavalry, a Jew came galloping out from behind a large boulder. He was obviously one of their leaders, staying behind to make sure as many of his men as possible had escaped before making his own dash for freedom. He wore a bright red cloak, masking his face, and dark curly hair.

The Romans gave a great shout as he appeared, but he was instantly at the gallop, while they had slowed their mounts back to a canter once they saw the rescue was made. Marcus considered making a try at stopping the man, but thought better of it; Mithras had brought him safely through, when all the odds had been against it. No man risked his life on throwing Venus twice on successive casts of the dice. Let him go.

The only person who stood between the Zealot and safety was the wife of the merchant. And she stood there because fear had given roots to her feet. As the rider swept down on her, she threw her gown up over her head, in a reflex action of pure fright, showing her skinny shanks, streaked with dirt.

The Jew swung a loop of rope as he rode, and he cast it at the woman, instantly taking a turn about the pommel of his saddle. It dropped nearly over her shoulders, and for a moment it seemed as though it might simply fall clean over her to the floor. But the Gods were not on her side that day, and it tightened around her knees, jerking her off her feet.

She had time for one terrified cry, then the momentum of the horse began to pull her along the ground. Feet first. Her arms trailing after her, as she tried desperately to keep her head and face off the rocks. But the strain was too great, and even before she'd gone out of sight, she was beginning to leave a trail of blood over the stony soil.

Marcus watched it happen, and knew there was nothing he could do. He'd seen similar things happen in the arena. There had been a mighty gladiator, past his prime when Marcus had seen him, called Pallantius. Who fought with net and trident. But he fought from a chariot, keeping the loop of the net curled round his wrist, and knotted to the reins. His speciality was to entangle some poor secutor in the meshes of his net, and drag him round the amphitheatre until the body was merely bloody pulp.

He was a great favourite of the crowds, but not with the attendants of the arena, whose job it was to clean up the sand after each combat. It was said that they needed ten times the sand when Pallantius fought.

He'd died, finally, by the same savage method. Losing his edge through age, and still insisting on fighting, he had let his net get entangled with the wheels of his own chariot, and he'd been dragged to his own death.

And the crowd had never laughed as much as on that day!

They didn't find the body of the woman, though a patrol

followed the smears of blood, watching them turn to trails of brains, then splinters of bone as all the blood was mashed from the corpse. Finally, there was nothing left to wear down, and the sand grew softer. So they turned back.

Another patrol went on, casting round in a large circle, and they pulled in a fish with their net. A tall man, with dark curly hair. Wearing a red cloak.

Marcus had finished his report, and had said a fond farewell to the Lady Agrippina, promising to take care and return safely. He was spared a meeting with her husband, who was out with a party of tribunes on a hunting expedition. She had called him to their tent, and had kissed him hard on the lips, letting her hot little tongue probe into his mouth. Then she had let him go. But the promise of the help as a gladiator was there. And it was a promise that he intended to hold.

A soldier stopped him, telling him that they'd taken a prisoner, and would he go to the tent of the Praefectus Castrorum. He was the senior of the professional soldiers. A short, squat man, running to fat, named Octavius Antoniarus. Although there were those who liked him, claiming he was a fine soldier, Marcus had never liked him. Sharing the more popular belief that Antoniarus was not to be trusted.

'Come in, young Marcus. Good piece of work you did there. If Old Big Tits had died, there'd have been the devil to pay. Hear you also had a bit of trouble with some black gladiator. Tell me about it tomorrow, will you? I've . . . got a lot on tonight, you know.'

Marcus did. Antoniarus's affairs with his slave woman was the scandal of the Legion. There was no future to it, as the word would eventually get to Flavius Silva, and he would break him for his way of life.

'I'm glad the Lady Agrippina was pleased with what little I could do,' he said, keeping his voice neutral.

'Bet you managed more than a little, you young dog, Marcus. Still. That's not why you're here. My men caught one of those stinking Jews. Says he wasn't on the raid, and that he's not a Zealot. But my Centurion says that one of them had a bright red cloak. This man's got a cloak of that colour. I'll have him brought in.' He shouted out to his sentry, and there was the sound of marching feet. 'Did you get a good look at him?'

Before Marcus could answer, an escort stamped into the tent, half-dragging a man between them. Tall, with curly hair, hanging low over the nape of his neck. He was naked above the waist, and his cloak, whatever colour it might have been, was gone. The soldiers let go of him, giving him a push so that he fell face down on the floor of the tent. The lights had guttered as they brought him in, and his head had hung down, so that Marcus had still not had the chance to see his face. Yet, there was something oddly familiar about the man. It certainly looked like the man who had ridden through them, and who had dragged off the merchant's wife to her death.

His back showed that Antoniarus had put him to the question, salting the interrogation with a flogging. The whip of one of the Centurions had doubtless been used. The thongs of leather with their rows of tight, tiny knots, some with a small ball of lead tied in. But the Praefectus had not been too severe. The mere fact that the Jew was still alive showed that. Fifty lashes with a Legion whip, and the bones and nerves of the spine became exposed and the man collapsed and died.

'I felt it might be of some use, if he is the man, to take our time. Perhaps he knows a way that the nut of Masada can more easily be cracked. And after that I thought that such a big fellow might do well in the Circus.'

Marcus hadn't the least concern with the Jew, except to see him dead. If it was the man, and it looked uncommonly like him, then he had caused the death of several Roman soldiers, as well as nearly killing Marcus himself. And if it wasn't him . . . Well, if it wasn't him, then life was far too short to worry about all the men and women and children who died for the wrong reason during a war.

Anxious to get back to his own tent and snatch some sleep before he departed at dawn for Masada, Marcus gave the figure a casual kick, ready to go through the motions of identifying him. Stirring under his foot, the Jew rolled half over and looked up at him.

It was Samuel ben Ezra.

The scenes in the wine-shop flashed back to Marcus, as he gazed down at the battered face of the boy who had rescued him from certain death. The soldiers had done a fine job with the Jew. His eyes were both half-closed and purple, and it looked as though they'd broken his nose. A black thread of blood ran from the corner of his mouth, past swollen lips.

'Well?'

He realized that the Praefectus must have asked him whether this was the Jew who had led the attack. He hesitated for a moment. His father had drilled into him that the first loyalty of a Roman was to Rome and the Empire. But his mother had always told him to balance his affections. And that to her the first loyalty was to one's family. Then to one's friends. Then to Rome.

He thought about those loyalties, and how their life had been ruined despite the way they'd each tried to live by their own standards. The other thing that his father had told him was to pay his debts. And there could be few greater debts than to a man who had saved your life.

'Come on! I haven't got all night. Tell me it's the man and we'll get on with things.'

'No.'

'No?'

'No, Praefectus. That's definitely not the man I saw today. He was shorter, and older. This fellow – what one can see of him after your men have had their sport – is barely as old as I am.'

Antoniarus was taken aback by the denial. His mouth opened and shut twice, and he waved his arms in the air. 'Not him?'

'Not him. It looks as though he's already paid a high price just for being a Jew and wearing a red cloak.'

'I'll have him beaten again, as a warning, and then taken from the city.'

The little man turned in a swirl of cloak and self-esteem, pausing at Marcus's cough. 'Well? What is it this time?'

'With the greatest respect, sir. Was it not the order of the Emperor himself that we should try and avoid upsetting those Jews who were not part of the revolt? There is only a handful of the Zealots at Masada. The city here is in ruins, though they try daily to rebuild a little. There can be no harm in encouraging this, now the dogs have learned their lesson. An incident with this man could cause a new feeling of rebellion.'

On the floor, ben Ezra looked up at him, his face immobile.

Antoniarus breathed heavily, scratching his nose with the tip of one chubby finger. 'Well. I suppose there might be something in what you say, young Marcus. Yes. I suppose the sight of a boy in this condition might cause comment.' He hesitated. 'That is, supposing he really is innocent, and that you're not mistaken. After my men saw that stray horse galloping out of the pass with half a dozen arrows in it, they came at the gallop. But none of them actually saw the leader's face.'

'I am certain that it is not the man,' said Marcus, hoping that the shades of the dead soldiers would not be too offended by his lie.

'So you say. So you say. Enough of this. I am eager to avoid trouble. The Legates have been complaining of the rough treatment of some of these animals, and this lad might make things worse for me.'

Marcus risked a wink at Samuel, masking his relief from the officer.

'Good. Marcus. I make you responsible for him. Take him out in the desert and kill him. Take a detail and get the body well buried. You may carry on.'

'No!' Marcus stared angrily at the shocked face of his superior officer. 'No, that wasn't what I meant. Praefectus, it would do well for you and for your career if it were known that you made your decisions based on wisdom and humanity as well as on strength and force. The Lady Agrippina will hear of this Jew, and she has a heart filled with warmth.'

Antoniarus was about to make a ribald comment, then checked himself as he remembered that Marcus was, if the reports were true, somewhat close to the lady. He waved the youth to go on.

'I know that she would be pleased to hear of your compassion towards this innocent man, Praefectus. And would hasten to tell her husband. And he in turn would take the words to the General himself. And all for one pathetic Jew.'

The hook was well planted, and Marcus stood back, content to watch. Antoniarus was not a fool, despite his absurd infatuation for his slave woman. He knew that there was talk. Not just about the liaison – that was nothing. But whispers that he was neglecting the running of the camp for the woman. That could prove fatal if it reached the ears of Flavius Silva.

'Well enough then, Marcus. You know how to appeal to my soft old heart. Tell the Lady Agrippina, won't you? Let him go free. See to it. Farewell.'

There was the clashing of salutes, and then he was gone, with the escort following him out. Marcus was left alone with the Jew, who slowly staggered to his feet, looking at his saviour without speaking.

'You killed many of my fellows, Samuel ben Ezra,' said Marcus, keeping his voice low so that the sentries wouldn't hear him.

'Aye, Roman. As I slew many of my fellows to save you.'

It was a fair comment, and Marcus felt a little ashamed of himself. The Jew had obviously taken a bad beating, and could hardly stand, and Marcus pointed to a chair in the corner of the tent.

'How did they catch you?'

'I dragged that woman until I tired of it – I hope she wasn't one of your women, Marcus Julius Britannicus? No? Good. And I lost contact with the others of my band. So your soldiers caught me alone and with a tired horse.'

There was an uneasy silence between them. Then the young Jew laughed quietly. 'I have to admire the way you handled that strutting little dung-hill cockerel. The one with the soft heart!'

Marcus laughed. 'The soft heart of Antoniarus is well renowned in the camp of the Tenth Legion. He weeps as he watches men hanged, or women split apart by teams of horses, or children thrown on to fires.'

'Or temples razed to the ground at the whim of a tyrant who lives hundreds of your miles from here!'

There was a great bitterness in his voice, and Marcus looked at him. 'It was not my doing, brother. And there had been much slaughter on your side as on ours.'

Looking cautiously at the closed flap of the tent, ben Ezra got up and walked to stand near the young Roman. 'It is true, my brother. So, lest we fall to fighting between each other, let us have no talk of the rights and wrongs of this matter.'

And they clasped hands again on it.

Later that night, after the surgeon had seen to Samuel's injuries, they went together to the guarded gate of the camp, where Marcus was to see him clear of the soldiers. Samuel walked a few paces away, then came back again, his eyes staring deep into Marcus's.

'There is a thing that I have not said. And I say it now. I thank you, Marcus. You saved my life, and I thank you for it.'

'It was a debt.'

'Aye. I like not these debts that men lay upon each other. I fear they come between friendship. Yet, the debt was there. And now it has gone.'

Behind them, the guard was changing, and they could hear the shouts of the soldiers as they ran to get their meal of soup and bread. With cheese and an apple if they were in luck. The Porta Praetoria – the main gate of the camp – was heavily protected, standing as it did, close under what was left of the old city wall.

Marcus walked a few paces away from the gate with Samuel. Until they reached the edge of the ring of light cast by the torches. Then he stopped.

'It is as well, Samuel. Perhaps we shall meet again.'

'Perhaps.' There was an odd smile playing around the puffed lips of the young man. 'Perhaps we may meet again. I wonder whether the Gods intend us to be linked in this way. And maybe we shall never see each other again.'

'That would sadden me.'

'And me. We are much of an age, Marcus. You are, what, near seventeen?'

'Yes. And you?'

'The same. But, now I must go. As must you. You go to join your famous general.'

'At Masada. You?'

'I go to join my friends.'

'Where?'

Samuel had nearly vanished in the darkness, but his words floated back clearly. 'Where else but at Masada? Yes, brother, at Masada.'

And he was gone.

FIVE

Masada. There was a rock, not small in its circumference, and very high. It was surrounded with valleys of such astounding depth downwards that the eye could not perceive their floors. They were so steep that no animal could walk upon them, except at two places of the rock, where it subsides, in order to afford a passage for ascent, though this be exceedingly difficult. On these paths, there is nothing but destruction should your feet slip, for on all sides there are vast chasms and precipices that are sufficient to suppress the courage of any man by the very terror that it places in the mind ... Upon the very summit of this mighty hill did Jonathan the High Priest first of all build a fortress. And he did call it by the name of 'Masada'.

From the 'Works Of Flavius Josephus',
37–100 (?) A.D.

'There it is. We've been here for nearly nine months, and for the first time, I really believe that the end of the affair is near to hand. I pray to the Gods each night that it is. I can't stand much more of this damned heat.'

Marcus stood with the young Legate, gazing up in awe at the fortress of Masada, fifty miles south-east of Jerusalem, overlooking the placid waters of the Dead Sea. It was truly a daunting sight, and he could understand the feeling of defeat that had come to the Tenth Legion when they'd first arrived in the previous year. And the exaltation they must now be feeling as they saw their labours coming inexorably towards their end.

It was unbelievably hot in the desert, with the sun hanging like a bowl of molten gold, suspended between the surrounding mountains. And the fortress dominating the scene. It stood well over a thousand feet high, and there were, it was said, only two ways up. And both were guarded by Zealots.

'Trouble is, Marcus Britannicus, the paths are so damned narrow that an old woman armed with a willow staff could hold off a whole Legion.'

'But the siege must be taking a dreadful toll of the Jews up there. How many are there?'

'We don't exactly know. That's where your mission'll come in useful, if you can get in. And if you can get back again in one piece. The last spy they caught up there they cut up and threw down to us a bit at a time. Took a week for it all to reach us. We think about a thousand. Men, women and a few brats. The place up there is supposed to have huge storehouses, still full of food.'

'Water?'

The Legate shaded his eyes against the sun and pointed up at the red-brown flank of the mountain. 'Aaah. That was where old Flavius Silva thought we'd got them. There's those aqueducts, bringing water from the other hills. That'd be no good, but it seems that they've got massive holes hollowed out in the middle of the rock. The Jews must have laboured like rabbits to get it done. Those holes are the openings to a system of culverts and cisterns. That's what stores the water.'

'Rain?' In the weeks he'd been out there, Marcus had not even seen a single drop of rain. And the sky was its usual cloudless blue.

'Aye. Twice in the last few months we've had rain. And such rain! Like nothing you've ever seen. Although your father was from Britain, and I hear it always rains up there, doesn't it?'

At the mention of his father, and of Britain, Marcus had automatically steeled himself for an insult or a sneer, but the Legate was obviously making a simple and innocent remark. They didn't always.

It had only been a year or so back that a group of young officers were gambling and drinking and one of them had seen Marcus enter. There had been words spoken. Loud enough for him to hear. Deliberately so. Sneering. He had gone to the officer and asked him if he would repeat the words. When he had refused, for the fighting reputation of Marcus was well known, he had called him a coward and slapped him hard across the face.

Encouraged on by his fellow patrician officers, the young man had risen and walked out, followed by Marcus. They had gone round the back of the wine-shop, and the others had remained behind. Becoming more sober as they waited, for the youth with Marcus was the son of a senator, and carried great influence.

After a few minutes, Marcus had walked back in, unmarked, and told them to go and fetch their friend. They had found him stretched against a wall, with both eyes pulped to bloody jelly. His father had been told of a murder by natives, and everyone had kept quiet. Thinking of the honour of the Legion. And of the safety of their own skins for having been concerned in the affair.

After that, there had been less and less of the sneering, thanks also to the intervention of Flavius Silva. And now Marcus stood below the walls of Masada, the fort upon the rock, with a commission from the General himself to try and enter Masada and find out what their disposition was, and how their spirits ran.

Ignoring the fact that he hadn't answered his question, the Legate went on. 'The rain falls down faster than a whore's drawers. And heavier than old Flavius's tongue when he's in one of his rages. The sky turns black and it pours out of those holes like a fountain, showering clean down the side of the mountain. And that's when they fill up their culverts.'

Marcus stared up at the walls. And then down to the earthworks that surrounded it. His fingers went up to his lucky stone, worn smooth by his constant touching. He tried to remember what he knew of military tactics, and he could see that Flavius Silva had done everything he could to try and crack this most difficult of nuts. The camp where he now stood was on the western side of the rock, and the main buildings, he knew, lay on the left as he looked at it. On the northern rim of Masada. Although there was a wall clear round the top, there had been attempts to rush the paths, but the Legate was right. There was no way up them past the determined defenders. And if there was no path up that the Romans could use? Then what could they do?

The answer was simple.

Using a multitude of labour, the Romans built another path. Shifting thousands of tons of rock and earth, they had built a massive ramp up the west side of the fortress, and it steadily inched its way towards the top.

'Another few days, and we shall be ready to plunge into that place and there will be nothing any of their pagan Gods can do to stop us. Five. Perhaps four days.'

The General's eyes had lit up at the thought. The fort had been an open ulcer in the flank of the Empire since it was captured from them some six years previously. And now it was going to fall. And it would fall to him. And the reputation of Flavius Silva was assured.

'How will you get in there? Someone said that he thought, and pardon me for repeating this, that you looked a bit like a Jew yourself, and that you could somehow smuggle yourself in and pass yourself as one of the Zealots.'

Marcus wondered that himself. The paths were impossible. That great ramp was not yet near enough to the top. He wiped sweat from his brow, cursing the order that kept them all in armour when they were within slingstone range of the rock. But he had seen a soldier killed with a stone. No bigger than the egg of a hen, yet it had burst his skull apart, splattering his brains all over the baked earth. He looked up at the sky, wondering if they'd get any rain that might cool the place down, and saw a small cloud, tipping the horizon, no bigger than a maid's brooch.

'Will that bring rain?' he asked, pointing at it.

'Perhaps. They begin like that, and sometimes they go away and sometimes they get bigger. With this light wind it'll be near midnight before it reaches us anyway.'

He looked at the preoccupied expression on the face of the young scout, wondering if all the tales about his fighting skill were true. And if his father had truly been the traitor some men said. Flavius Silva might be a hard leader, but he was a fair one. He'd been prepared to give the boy a chance, so maybe he *was* all right. Certainly looked capable enough.

'What are you thinking, Marcus Britannicus? Wondering if you can hook a ride on a cloud that'll float you into their fortress?'

Marcus smiled at the laughter. 'If I told you what I was thinking, then you might laugh all the more. Leave me here. It's very nearly time for the meal, and I want to sit here and look at Masada, and think how I might fly into it.'

The Legate laughed at him, and marched off, his heavy sandals raising a puff of dust at each step. Left alone, Marcus again stared up at the rock face, paying particular attention to those holes, which he had been told were outflow vents for their water system. Over his head, the sun slowly dropped away behind the hills, and the darkness crept towards him from over the glittering bowl of the Dead Sea. And the darkness brought the clouds, lowering over the stars, and masking the country in a black veil.

It was a fine night for a murder. Or for a secret raid on an invulnerable fortress.

Once, he and his father had gone on a long hunting trip, accompanied only by Argos and a bare dozen soldiers and slaves. They'd ridden westwards from the sea, across the trackless forests of Britain, through Durobrivae, and over the central plain to Viroconium. There, they were entering the lands of the Ordovices, and they picked up an extra military escort into the mountains. They'd gone as far as Segontium, not risking any further exploration of the wild peninsula of Ganganorum.

It had been among the hills, snow-capped, though it had been near the end of winter, that Marcus had gone climbing, under the tuition of Argos. They'd scrambled up a sheer face, hanging on by toes and nails, bodies pressed to the cold rocks as the howling furies of the freezing wind tried to pluck them off and dash them to their deaths on the scree a thousand feet below. Marcus had been terrified, and exhilarated, all at the same time, and he had always regretted that they never repeated the expedition, and he was never again to travel lightheartedly over the damp, green land with his beloved father. Never again.

His foot slipped, and he hung for a dizzy moment by the fingers of his right hand, until he could regain a toehold. He cursed himself for losing his concentration, and letting his mind wander back to the days that were now only ashes of a near-forgotten fire. What was dead was dead, and it was now only important to live for the day.

The binding on the cloak was coming loose, and the wind was nibbling at an exposed edge of the dark wool, threatening at any moment to tear it away, setting it flapping about his head. Yet he couldn't rest to set it to rights. The words of old Argos came back to him, and he could almost hear that husky voice, and see the face, with the puckered skin round the wounded eye.

'Keep two hands and a foot on. Or two feet and a hand. Never less, if you want to lay another maiden in the straw when your mother's not watching.'

Even if there hadn't been the low cloud scudding over the moon, he doubted if he would now be able to see the earth, shimmering far below him. The rock wasn't quite as sheer as it had looked. There was no way that any large force could have made the climb. By night it would have been utterly impossible for them to keep together. By day they could have been picked off by a handful of children who would merely have needed to have rolled down a few stones to send every attacker crashing to a fearful death.

Because of the impossibility of the scheme, the Zealots seemed as though they weren't protecting that side, beyond the normal guards that Marcus had been told patrolled the top of the fortress. Far below him, and to his right, he could see the torches of the camp, glittering like tiny sparks in the blackness. While he was still on the lower slopes of the hill he had even been able to hear some men singing one of the bawdy songs of the Legion. Concerning a certain Centurion and a lobster, and the odd adventures that arose when they travelled together to Rome to see the ladies. He'd found himself humming the chorus as he scrambled over the loose rock, moving as quietly as he could towards the steeper face.

Now the wind had risen, and he could hear nothing from the camp. He managed to reach a small ledge, about a hundred feet below the summit, as he judged, and he tucked the cloak back into its wrapping. He wore a plain tunic of the type that most of the Zealots were dressed in. Woollen, with a broad belt that carried a simple dagger in a leather sheath.

For a moment he thought that he could hear voices above

him, but the main paths were on the far side of the mountain, and he guessed that it was a freak of the wind carrying up a snatch of conversation from below him. From his review of the face during the afternoon, he thought that he must be somewhere near the mouths of the culverts, where he hoped to climb in and hide.

The blast of thunder was so loud and seemed so close that Marcus came within a fraction of losing his grasp on the rock and plummeting down to his doom. The crack of lightning burned across his eyes, and he closed them, hanging on to his handholds, bracing his body against the face. The sandstone felt rough to his fingers, and tiny pieces of it rolled away, falling like dust into space.

The next flash was even closer, and he wondered if it had actually struck Masada. The tang of ozone filled the air, and his hair seemed to crackle on his skull. Thunder rolled around him, making his ears sing, overflowing the precipice and bouncing back in echoes from other hills.

Opening his eyes, he squinted around, trying to see where the mouths of the cisterns were. The brightness of the light had left him with a residual red glow, burning at the back of his eyes. The wind had risen, flattening him against the sun-warmed rock. There was a third flash, and a fourth and fifth. Gradually his sight cleared, and he was able to use the lightning to see where he was and where he wanted to go. Above him, and slightly to his left, was the gaping mouth of one of the caverns. To reach it he had to move like a crab, along the slope, knowing that there was a sheer drop of several hundred feet yawning below him.

The wind was now rising fast to a gale, tugging at his clothes, and making every single move a hazard. But at last he found himself safe in the shadow of the hole, and he was able to reach up and grasp the lip.

At that moment, it began to rain. Pattering off his head and back, bouncing in red lumps off the rock into his face. Rain such as Marcus had never seen before. It had rained often enough in Britain. Damp, driving drizzle that swept in low off the sea, over the flats and estuaries and soaking through into a man's bones.

But this rain! It fell in solid masses, filling his hair and ears and eyes with its screaming force. As it fell back off the rocks, it carried with it a sludge of red sand that poured into his mouth nearly drowning him. His tunic was weighed down with rain, dragging him backwards off the cliff.

His fingers scrabbled at the edge of the outlet, trying to lever himself up and in. But the years of water flowing over the stone had worn it down until it was as slippery as glass, and it seemed as though he would never do it. His legs felt like jelly, and Marcus knew that he was not going to be able to stand there for much longer before the strength seeped from his body and he simply toppled backwards, sliding down for a hundred feet or so, gradually going faster. Fingernails breaking and flesh ripped raw. Then he would be over the sheer brink of the precipice and falling free, the breath torn from him, until he was smashed to bloody flesh and bare bones on the boulders far below.

One of his favourite games as a child, in the long evenings when his parents were entertaining guests, was to compose short epigrams, modelled after Catullus. A poet that many matrons would have banned for a boy as young as he was, but his mother enjoyed the earthy quality of the poet, and encouraged him to read.

And there, plastered to the rock wall of Masada, one of his sayings came back to him. 'Endeavour will carry you through the times of little hope better than hope will carry you through times of little endeavour.'

It was truly a time of little hope, with the storm growing in fierceness, and his clothes weighing him down more and more. He drew in a deep breath of the cool, fresh air, and then thrust up, like an arrow leaving the string, pushing off both footholds at once, his hands reaching for the overhanging lip of the cistern, finding it, and hanging on. His toes scratched at the rock, the leather of the sandals kicking away small chunks of the soft stone in his endeavour.

And it worked. There was the hint of a foothold and he was able to lever himself up enough to slide inside, feeling the instant relief of being out of the wind and the rain. The one problem was that nobody in the Roman camp had the least idea how deep the tanks were, and how far he would have to fall to reach the bottom. Inside, the light from the storm hardly raised more than a flicker, and Marcus couldn't even guess at how far it was. It was even possible that it was a hundred feet down, and he would let go and drop to lie a mangled corpse for all eternity.

'Never gamble with your life, unless there are no other roads open to you,' Argos used to say. To leave himself weaponless in the heart of the Zealot fortress seemed madness, but the only thing he had that he could drop to learn the floor height was his dagger. If he didn't use it, and dropped, then he would still have his weapon, but he might be dead.

There was also his lucky pebble, but it never even crossed his mind to use that. Hanging on to the rim of the opening with one hand, he fumbled and dragged out the knife from the wet sheath, holding it out at arm's length and letting it fall. There was the briefest pause before he heard it strike with a dull thud on a stone floor. It sounded as though it was only a few feet.

And it was.

His sandalled feet slapped on the rough floor with a flat crack that horrified him, but it had been impossible to judge his landing exactly in the blackness. Fortunately, the storm seemed to be directly overhead and there was an almost continuous rumbling and crashing of thunder, making it sound as though there were giants on top of the mountain rolling huge boulders together.

Hands outstretched, fumbling over the dry stone, Marcus quickly found his dagger and stuck it in his belt again. Unrolled his wet cloak, and spread it out to dry, placing it near a vertical wall so that he could rest on it.

Then, all he could do was wait until it grew lighter and he could see if there was a way out of the cistern. If there wasn't . . . If there wasn't, then he doubted if he'd ever be able to make the climb back down again. Not even with all the endeavour in the world.

One of Marcus's great skills was to be able to relax no matter what the danger was. Since there was nothing he could do by staying awake, it was common sense that he should sleep. And so he did.

Outside, the rain continued to beat down with unrelenting force. On all the hills around Masada, it lay in pools, dribbling into streams. Rushing through gulleys into small rivers that quickly became foaming torrents. The aqueducts into the beleaguered fortress overflowed with the volume of water that ran into them. From those pipes, the water entered the complex system of water-carrying ducts and culverts that had been designed when Herod first built Masada as his palace.

The first that Marcus knew of all this was when he heard the noise of water bubbling against the floor, and suddenly felt it rising about his legs. With an exclamation, he leaped to his feet, picking up his cloak, still sodden, and leaned his back against the wall. The noise of splashing increased, and he could actually feel it getting higher. Reaching his ankles, and then creeping up his calves, even as he stood there.

Outside, the thunder had stopped, and there were no further flashes from the lightning to show him what the situation was in the cistern. This was one enemy that Marcus had no way of fighting, and all he could do was stand there and wait. And see just how high the water was going to rise.

It reached his knees, and was now gushing in faster than before.

From the noise, the torrent seemed as though it was coming in from the top corner of the tank, somewhere up to Marcus's right. Carefully, feeling with his hand against the wall, and probing at the floor with his outstretched foot, he began to move round his prison. The walls were smoother than the floor, with the gouge marks of the builders' chisels still there. They were completely vertical, with not a prayer of a handhold, and no ledge of any kind.

He ducked as he felt his way under the weight of water cascading in through the channel somewhere up in the ceiling. It beat down on his head, almost forcing him to his knees with its power. Then he was past it, and moving on the third side. As far as he could judge, the cistern was about fifteen paces square, and the roof sounded as though it could be as much as thirty feet in height.

By now, his movements were slower as the water reached the hem of his tunic and began to climb his thighs. For a moment, the black germ of panic attacked him, and he tried to move faster, almost falling from the wall and losing all sense of direction. Then he realized what was happening and deliberately stopped walking, and leaned back against the wall, fingering the stone of Boadicea, and calming his breathing as Argos had always told him.

It was only when he was halfway round the third side that a thought struck him. There must be times when the cisterns needed cleaning out. And that had to be done . . .

'Mithras!! From inside!'

His shout almost drowned out the thunder of the water as it poured in the dark room. Or, was it quite as dark as it had been? There seemed the faintest patch of grey smearing high up on the opposite wall. The hole that he'd come in through showed the first trace of the morning light.

Hope redoubled, Marcus pressed on further round the chamber, until his hand finally found what he'd hoped for. There was a staircase, the steps hewn from the living rock, up the wall where he stood. He found it with his hand, and quickly clambered up on it, going up several steps before he was clear of the water. Just before he found the stairs, the chill had climbed nearly to his waist. And it showed not the least sign of stopping.

Squatting on the rough stone, Marcus peered across through the black until he could make out the round shape of the outlet. From where he was, he judged it to be only a couple of feet from the top of the cistern. He'd hung from it by his hands and dropped. The water now stood at nearly four feet deep. Before it reached the opening, it had to rise to over twelve feet.

But at its present rate, it wasn't going to take all that long to get that high. He breathed a great sigh of relief that he'd found the way out. Otherwise . . . Once the water reached the top, then anything – or anyone – in it would be whirled round and dashed from the opening by the pressure of the water, and hurled clean over the edge of the mountain.

Marcus whistled his relief, and began to carefully climb the stairs, squeezing himself against the wall to lessen the risk of slipping and toppling back into the bubbling depths. At the top, there was a massively heavy door made of metal-bound wood, and with hinges thicker than a man's thigh. He realized it would take him all his strength to shift it, and he pressed his back to the task with all of his might.

Then found that it was locked.

There were two steps before the water got to the top. Marcus sat on the topmost step, staring moodily down at the frothing whirlpool below him. Outside, through the opening, the sun dazzled into the cistern, bursting in a mass of splintered diamonds of light as it hit the tumbling fall. It was ironic that it should be yet another sweltering day out there, while the rain from the night continued to gush along the complex system of aqueducts to fill the tanks of Masada. And there was no slowing of the rate.

The door was clearly designed to be waterproof, and keep the precious liquid safely contained. Marcus's plight was simple. The water would rise until he was forced to swim. Very soon after that, it would spill over the brim of the hole through which he'd entered. Like milk through a holed bucket, it would gush out with increasing force, and it would carry him out with it, since there was no kind of handhold on the smooth sides of the safety-valve.

His father would have appreciated the irony of it. He'd always liked the way the Gods played their little jests with human ambition. That had been in the old days before he became bitter and withdrawn. Now here was his son, on a mission for Rome of great personal danger. To break into a fortress that a whole Legion had failed to take. And Marcus had done it. He was inside. In a room that would soon become the means of his own death.

Idly, Marcus picked at a loose piece of plaster on the wall, resting his head against the massive door. When he heard movement, and felt the wood vibrate slightly. Although it was immensely thick, it sounded almost as though someone was drawing great bolts back.

So. Perhaps it was to be life after all. But only until whoever was out there realized that he could only have got in from outside and raised the alarm. But it was a chance of life, and Marcus muttered his thanks to Mithras as he drew the knife from his sheath, and held it ready. Point uppermost, prepared for the stab and quick move out the moment the door opened.

Slowly, silently, on what must be greased hinges, the door inched open. The light from the sun now filled the chamber, and Marcus stood to the side of the small platform at the top of the steps so that he could take the first man through the opening. The water swilled round his feet, but he hardly noticed the cold, as the excitement fired through him. He wasn't to die either the miserable death of a rat drowning in a trap, nor the appalling end of being sucked out and vomited from the top of the cliff as part of the waterfall. If he was to die, then it might be with his blade in his hand, and the blood of an enemy warm on his arms.

To his surprise, the door didn't open the whole way, stopping once it was ajar enough for one person to slip through. Better and better, thought Marcus. Let them come at me one at a time and I will slay them the same way. An arm was in the doorway, and then one of the Jews stood there, gazing down at the turbulent water.

Dazzled momentarily by the light gleaming off some ornament the man wore, Marcus grabbed at him, throwing him down over his knee in a wrestler's hold, the knife poised to slice open the Zealot's throat. He was taken aback at the lightness of the figure. And even more surprised when he smelled the scent on the body, and felt long hair drift over his feet. And heard the strangled gasp of fear.

'By Mithras!' he exclaimed. 'A sound, Jewess, and you are dead.'

But he had to kill her anyway. As quickly as he could. Ready for the next one who would be waiting outside. In the golden light of the sun, he could see that she was young, with hair as black as the wing of a raven, and eyes wide and brown like a frightened deer.

Her mouth hung open, and he noticed that there were crumbs of unleavened bread stuck to her lips. It was clearly time at Masada for the first meal of the day, breaking the night's fast. Perhaps she was alone.

'Are you alone? Answer me. Are you alone?'

She shook her head, and whispered something in a voice hoarse with shock. In what he thought must be the Jewish tongue. He still held her tightly, her back arched like a drawn bow over his knee, the point of his knife drawing a tiny bead of blood from her pulsing throat.

'If you weren't alone, then I would think your friends would have come to you by now. So.' He paused for a moment, turning away from the doorway, so that she hung half over the water, which still thundered into the echoing cistern. It would help to get rid of the body.

'I am sorry, girl. Your leaders should have surrendered to the might of Rome. I know not why they did not.'

The knife was poised, ready to slide through her neck, when he heard a voice from right behind him, speaking quietly in his ear.

'They do not give in, brother Marcus, because they prefer beans and freedom to cakes and slavery.'

The edge of a sword lay cold across the side of Marcus's throat, and he kept very still.

SIX

Carefully, Marcus released the girl, standing up, not turning round to face ben Ezra. He put the dagger back in its sheath, and stood still, hands down by his side, waiting for the young Zealot to make the next cast.

'Marcus Julius Britannicus. I had truly thought that the Gods would bring us together again. Yet I had pondered on how that might be. It was not likely that I would come again to your camp in our shadow. So it had to be that you would try and come here.'

'And now, Samuel, my brother, I am here. The dice lie by your hand. Will you take them up or no?'

'Would you have killed my sister, brother? Would you have drawn your knife through the neck of Rachel? Tell me that, and tell me what is true. I shall see if you lie to me, Marcus, and I will know.'

Marcus turned round carefully, looking at the short sword in the Jew's hand. Saw it shaking slightly with the tension of the moment. Looked deep into his eyes, and saw himself mirrored there, with the golden glow of the morning sun cascading all round him. And he gave him his answer.

'I knew not that she was your sister. How could I know that?'

'But would you have killed her? I have to know what was in your mind.'

He forced a smile. 'I would not have killed her, my brother. It was in my mind to silence her with a blow to the head. But I should not have killed her. Not for this fortress nor for all of the world.'

Samuel smiled back at him, his hand reaching out and touching him on the shoulder. 'I am glad to my heart of that, Marcus. For if it had not been so, then I would have slain you here like a dog.'

There seemed to be a lump in Marcus's throat and he swallowed hard to clear it. There had been a moment when the honest answer had trembled on the tip of his tongue, seeming to beg him to spit it out. But life was very sweet, and he had gambled and won.

Together the two men walked out of the chamber, with the girl leading them. During the rescue she hadn't spoken a word. Nor had she looked up at Marcus. It was clear that she spoke no Latin, and Marcus was glad of it. If she had understood what her brother had asked, and what he had answered, she would have betrayed him. She knew what he intended. She had felt the pressure of the knife and seen the look in his eyes just before Samuel appeared. She would know all her life that the Roman had meant to slay her.

Samuel muttered a few words to her, and she ran silently away, vanishing round a bend in the passage. He gestured to the door, and the two men leaned against it, and heaved it shut. Marcus was surprised how easily it closed, guessing that there had to be some sort of counter-weight to help.

'You were lucky, again, Roman. After the rain, it is the duty of the young women, those who are not yet given in marriage, to check all of the chambers for water. As they do each day for the chambers that hold the oil, the corn, the fruit, the wine. It happened that I followed her. I know not why. Perhaps the Gods might know. And there, cast up like a fish from a net, was this Roman spy.' Marcus made a slight gesture towards his knife, and Samuel put his hand on his arm. 'Forgive the word, my brother, but is that not what you are? Of course you are. And I think none the less of you for it. The question is: what are we to do about it?'

The corridor where they walked was narrow and cool, with paintings on the plastered walls, showing scenes of hunting and of women standing beside blue waters. They met nobody, though Marcus was somehow conscious of there being people about.

'You could set me on the Serpent path and let me through the guards. Or you could take me to your leader. Eleazar, is that his name?'

'Eleazar ben Ya'ir is our Commander. I think that I cannot simply let you go. If you had been caught some days ago, then you would have died. But now. . . .'

He let the sentence tail off into silence, stopping at a corner of the passage, looking at Marcus, his face sad.

'Now? What's so different now, brother? If you must give me up, then that is what you must do. The Fates govern us all, Samuel. I will not hold it against you.'

'Come with me.' Samuel led him quickly along twisting corridors, seeming to make his way upwards, and to the north. They occasionally passed windows, and Marcus saw the sun gleaming across the courts. He noticed that the wooden floors of many of the rooms they passed had been ripped out, presumably for fuel as the siege bit harder. They began to meet others, bustling about their business. At Samuel's word, Marcus donned his cloak, pulling it up round his face so that he would not be recognized as an outsider. The main problem was that he was clean-shaven, whereas nearly all of the men that they saw wore heavy beards.

Finally, Samuel showed him into a small room at the centre of a block of buildings. It was empty, but it was obviously the room where he and his sister lived. His red cloak hung over a small bed. Samuel sat down on a bed, motioning Marcus to sit on the other.

'I regret that I can offer you no fine wine or food, my brother. The supplies are not what they once were, and your General Silva has closed near all of the doors on us. When we met those few days past, it was our last raid to try and get food. We have water enough to hold out for ever, but the flour and oil is near spent. And your damned ramp grows higher each day for all we can do against it.'

There was an intense depression in the Zealot's voice, and Marcus realized that the end must truly be near for him to talk like this.

'Then why do you not yield and spare all the children and the women. We are not butchers, brother. We would spare the lives of all but the leaders. Most of your men, and all of the rest will live. Let me talk to your leader and then I can take his words to Flavius Silva and many might live who would otherwise die. What do you say?'

Samuel shook his head. 'Brother. If the world were left to you and me to set to rights, then there might be some hope for it. We know of your General, and what he has promised to do to us and to this place. He is a hard man, who will not rest until he has done what he has sworn to do. Eleazar is the same man. Cast in the same mould, only he is a Jew and not a Roman. He has sworn that there will never be final surrender to the cause of the Jews here in our land. It does not matter what passes here. You cannot kill every Jew in the country. There will be those who will live and who will carry on the torch. Though the Empire of Rome last a thousand years . . . or ten times a thousand years, this will still be our land. The land of the Jews, and we will always be here to fight for it and to die for it!'

His voice had become raised, and his eyes flashed with the power of his belief. Marcus sat in silence as he finished speaking, realizing that there was little he could do here that would be of help either to Samuel or to Rome. The sword had been out from its scabbard for too long. It could not now be sheathed until it was all over. And that would not be long.

'How many of you are there left, Samuel? If you wish not to tell me, then I shall understand.'

'No. There is no reason not to tell you. The day is nearly over for Masada, and night rushes towards us across the darkening plain. It is of no help to your General to know our numbers. He will know them soon enough when he counts our dead. There are nine hundreds and sixty and two of us. Some half are men, and the rest women and children. If we had more food we could do more. There is no shortage of weapons. We have swords and shields enough if there were ten thousands of us.'

It was true. Everyone down in the camp knew that the ramp could not fail. Inexorable, it crept higher. Once it reached the top the soldiers would pour over in a living flood of bloody death, and no power on earth could hold them back. Silva had said that it would be within the week. Perhaps sooner.

Marcus stood up and walked slowly round the room. 'Samuel. Is there no hope that I can talk to this Eleazar and at least get him to let the women and children go?'

'No.' Samuel shook his head. 'I think not. Yet, the time is now so close that I see scant harm in taking you to him. There is always the hazard that he will have you thrown off the top of the northern terraces, brother. But I will say that I brought you in secretly, and that you are an ambassador from the Romans come to ask for our terms. Aye, I think me that it might well serve. At least he will listen to you. He is a fair man, Eleazar, but hard.'

The two men stood beside each other; height for height and breadth for breadth they were nearly identical. They smiled at each other, and on a common impulse embraced.

'Samuel ben Ezra. That is twice that you have saved my life and twice put me in your debt. Once I have paid you, yet the debt is still there. I like this not.'

'Nay, Marcus. I like not to be the creditor for any man's life. If we both come through these days, then let us swear never again to save the other.'

Laughing, yet aware of what they had said, the two men went together to the rooms of the Commander of the Zealots on Masada. Eleazar ben Ya'ir.

He was a short man, broad, with the heavy muscles of a wrestler. Showing the first signs of going to fat, with a spreading middle under a plain brown tunic and cloak. There were other older men with him, standing talking in a crowded room near the north of the fortress.

Samuel introduced Marcus to Eleazar, and there was an instant response from the other Jews. There was snarling, and more than one hand dropped to a sword-hilt. They ceased when their Commander raised a hand. His voice was surprisingly mild, but Marcus sensed the strength that lay close beneath the surface. It was true what Samuel had said. There was indeed a similarity between the Zealots' leader and the Roman General who opposed him.

'So. The mighty Flavius Silva sends beardless boys to do his work for him.'

The Latin was careful, but creaked a little, as though it had not been used overmuch for many years. Marcus bowed to him, keeping his face clean of any emotion. 'As the mighty Eleazar ben Ya'ir sends his youths to kill Romans,' pointing at Samuel ben Ezra.

The older man smiled a thin, quick smile. 'So. Well, my cockerel, what does our cousin have to offer us on this fine morning?'

'He wishes only to see an end of this battle. There is no other fighting in all of the land. Masada is truly the last outpost, and it will fall within the next few days, and there will be an end of it. Do you wish to have the deaths of so many upon your conscience?'

The Commander sat down, sighing, rubbing a bandage on his right shoulder. 'This damned wound will not heal. No matter. I shall meet my Maker with it, and I warrant he will not think any the less of me for it. You talk to me of death, do you? Come here, and let me see what you are.'

Warily, Marcus went to stand near him, but Eleazar reached out and pulled him closer, so that their faces were only inches apart. The Zealot had dark eyes, nearer to black than any Marcus had ever seen, with large pupils. He stared into Marcus's eyes for some moments without speaking, then pushed him gently away.

'You are a man for one so young, Marcus Britannicus. And I see that you do know of death. It is rare for me to see an officer of great Rome who is not a primping, perfumed eunuch. If I thought you were not a man, then I would have your throat slit, and have you fed to the birds. But you ask me what I wish, and I will answer you.'

Marcus stood back as Eleazar rose to his feet, and his eyes were suddenly afire, and his voice rose, filling the small room with its rich tones. In that moment, Marcus saw why Eleazar was such a feared leader, and why the chances of Flavius taking him alive were so remote. When the Progress came after the victory, there would be no Zealots in chains at the General's chariot tail.

'It is given to me to be the leader of these my people, dwelling under the heel of the Roman sandal. Cowering in the shadow of slavery. I shall lead my people from this, saith the Lord God. From bondage and from the scourge. It is better to die on your feet than to live for ever on your belly. If the great Flavius Silva lets us go, then he must let us all go from Masada. Every man and every woman and every child. With all our stock and all our weapons, and we shall then go and find another fortress to hold against the Romans, unless he leaves us quite at peace. Will he do this, Roman? Will he?'

There was only one answer, and everyone there knew it.

Marcus slowly shook his head. 'I am no child, Eleazar ben Ya'ir. I have seen many deaths, and killed many men, though I have but seventeen summers. It is not for me to tell you that your words are chaff thrown into the teeth of the wind.' There was an angry murmur, but the Zealot Commander merely watched him, unmoving. 'They are the babble of spring water over cold stones. They mean nothing, other than death for all here. I put it to you that we would spare the women and the children and most of the men.'

Marcus was wildly exceeding anything that he was there for, but the situation wasn't what he'd expected to find. Nor was it what Flavius Silva thought. All the Legion below was looking for a savage and bloody battle with the defenders screaming their defiance as they died.

But there was an odd spirit. Not one of defeat. More one of resignation. Marcus was unable to see where it would end, and he was like a man fishing in the dark, not sure where his hook would land, nor even what sort of fish he might bring up.

'Go on. It is only meet that we should all know what it is that your General has to say.' Eleazar's voice was now quieter, as though the fires of his spirit had been banked down, but simply slumbered, waiting only a chance wind to spring again to an all-consuming blaze.

'That is all. You offer death, and I offer life. Do you speak for your people? For all of them?'

For a moment, Marcus thought that he'd pushed the Zealot too far, and he let his hand drop to his side for the reassuring feel of the dagger hilt. It would have done little against so many, but it was better to die fighting than to be butchered.

'I give you my answer, and then you will go and take it to your General. Come with me.'

Led by the stooping figure of the Commander, with Samuel ben Ezra at his side, Marcus walked along corridors, coming out twice into the burning heat of the sun, into another block on the eastern side of the mountain, furthest away from the activity of the ramp. Over on that side there was smoke coming up from a fire, and the cry of men in action. Eleazar saw him pause, and stopped with him.

'They are your people, pushing harder to break through. They have managed to fire some of the buildings near the top of the hill they make. And the wall is breached by your stones. Yet it will hold for just a little longer. Come.'

They went into a smaller building, with most of its floors intact. It was crowded with beds, full of men lying like fish in a barrel, side by side by side. All wounded. The floor was clean, but the place stank of blood and excrement and of death.

"This is our hospital.' He stopped a man hurrying past, wearing a gown of red wool, that still showed the thick patches of blood on it. Eleazor spoke quickly to him, and the man shook his head. The Zealot pointed to Marcus, and the doctor, if that was what he was, turned and stared at him with an expression of bitter hatred. Then nodded, and beckoned them to follow him into a smaller room at the end of the passage.

At the door he paused, and said something to his leader. Eleazar translated it into his careful Latin for the benefit of Marcus. 'He says that he cannot have us all in there. Just you and me, and ben Ezra.' With something of a twinkle in his eye he looked at the young Roman. 'While we are in there, it would be easy for you to slay me. I will not threaten you with what would surely happen to you if you did. I merely ask that you give me your word that you will not.'

'You have it.'

'Come then.'

It was very hot in the room, and ill-lit, with a circle of lamps flickering away in the corners of the walls. The only furniture there was a long table, and a smaller bench at its side. On the bench Marcus saw a row of tools. Saws, hammers, chisels, needles and files. Knives, honed down to a thin edge.

Marcus took all this in at a glance, but his main attention was for the long table, and what lay on it. He couldn't even guess what sort of wood the table had once been. It was so soaked in old and fresh blood, and so cut about with what looked like sword scars. And on it lay a young girl, about fourteen if he was any judge of age.

She was rolling around, crying out quietly in pain, though she held a bloody rag between her lips to try and stifle her screams.

'If the others hear too much crying from here, they become downhearted,' explained Samuel in a whisper.

The girl saw Eleazar come in, and tried to sit up. As she did the dirty blanket covering her legs fell away to the floor, revealing what was beneath. Used as he was to the savage side of warfare, Marcus winced and looked away at the sight.

Her legs had been crushed, by what looked like one of the big stones hurled from the catapults the Romans had mounted on the ramp to help protect it from attack. The stones were round and as large as a man's head, thrown high in the air to crack down again with appalling force. The one leg was swollen purple, with red and yellow threads running through it where the infection had already taken hold. The ankle was twisted at a crooked angle and some of the toes were gone. The other leg was straight, and seemed less marked. Less marked until you looked more carefully near the top of the thigh, and saw the whiteness of a jagged piece of bone actually protruding through the torn flesh.

Eleazar gently eased the girl back, cushioning her head with his arm. He and the doctor exchanged a few words, which the Commander translated for the benefit of Marcus.

'She has been wounded by one of your . . .'

'I can see what has wounded her.'

'Well enough. She has infections and the humours have possessed both limbs. We do not have the skill nor the time here to save her. If she was taken down the mountain, then your surgeons could save her. No?'

'Possibly.'

'If she stays, we must cut off both her legs or she will be dead within a day. She knows this. She also knows that even with both her legs hacked away with that saw there, her chances are very faint. Do you understand?'

'Of course. The Roman way and she might live. The way of the Zealots and she will die. In great pain. And she chooses this, knowing what will happen?'

'Ask her. No, you cannot. If I ask her you might not trust me. You trust the word of ben Ezra? Samuel, ask her. Tell her this boy is going down to the camp of the Legions, and that there they might save her. And that we will do what we can, but she must lose both her legs, and probably her life if she remains. Tell her that.'

Glancing at Marcus, Samuel began to speak to the girl, wiping her brow with a cloth soaked in water as he did so. He had hardly begun when she began to shake her head, looking all the while at Marcus. She took the rag from between her teeth, and muttered a few hoarse words to Samuel.

'She wishes to give you her answer, Marcus. Come closer.'

Wincing at the stench and the flies that rose in a black cloud from her legs as he moved in closer, Marcus leaned across so that his face was near to the girl. Summoning up all her energy, she raised her face to his, and spat.

His reaction was instant and instinctive. He clenched his fist and struck her hard in the mouth, knocking her back so that her head cracked on the boards of the table, and she lay still. Blood flowed freely from a deep cut on her lip where his knuckle had caught her.

Marcus straightened up, wiping her sticky spittle from his cheek, feeling the growth of two days' stubble scratch at his fingers. He looked round at the watching Zealots, his eyes angry, ready to draw his knife if any of them spoke against what he'd done. But none of them did. The doctor was quickly assembling his saws, eager to take advantage of the girl's unconsciousness. Eleazar stood immobile, his arms folded, while Samuel looked away, not wishing to meet Marcus's eyes.

'So. That is your answer to Flavius Silva, is it? Very well, Eleazar ben Ya'ir. Give me your safe-conduct and I shall leave this place. And I will return tomorrow, before the sun has set.'

The Zealot Commander nodded his agreement, and Marcus left the small room. The last sound that he carried with him away from Masada was the grating of saw-teeth on bone, and the beginning of a bubbling moan of pain. Quickly stifled.

SEVEN

Flavius Silva, General in charge of the Tenth Legion besieging Masada, was very much like Eleazar, commanding the Zealots within the fortress. He heard Marcus's report with a grave face, asking questions about the defences of the mountain, most of which Marcus was able to answer. He was interested in the spirit of the defenders, pursuing this subject as much as any other. It was only when his young scout came to what he thought was the meat of the report, concerning the words of Eleazar, that Flavius seemed to lose interest.

'You've done well, Marcus Britannicus. Very well, and the Emperor shall hear of this in my next report. It may help to clear the name of your family. I will do what I can in that quarter.'

He waved a hand to dismiss the youth, but Marcus stood his ground. Flavius looked up at him with a trace of irritation. 'What is it, my boy? I'm very busy preparing for the attack tomorrow morning.'

'Tomorrow!'

'Yes. Tomorrow. Why? Do you want to be the first one through the breach when the ramp finally gets to the top? I'll arrange it if you want. But I have to tell you, Marcus, as an old soldier, that it is generally the second one through who collects the honour. The first one always gets the spears and arrows. That's something for you to remember. The second man gets to be the General. The first one simply gets to be dead.'

'No. No, sir, it's not that. It's that I gave my word as a Roman officer that I would return later today with your conditions for their surrender. Would you have me break my word to the Jews?'

'Blood of Mars!! Don't you come here and bait me in my own tent, Marcus, with what your word of honour means, or I'll forget my word to your father and break my staff across your backside. You went on that mission with orders to spy out the land up there and see what their spirits were like. Very well. You did that. And we know that they're like ripe peaches, just ready to fall into our fingers. I attack tomorrow morning at dawn, and if you want to go up there first, then it's on your own head. Do you?'

Marcus snapped to attention. 'I do, sir. With respect, I have given my oath to them. And if they should surrender, then it would look well. No losses on our side. Captives to lead in triumph.'

Flavius smiled. 'I'm too old a fish to catch like that. But it is true, and I see what you're getting at. But you've said the Zealots will never yield.'

'Eleazar might spare the women and the children from the final slaughter when we attack, sir. That's worth a try, isn't it?'

Flavius stood up. 'You're a man of honour, and you believe in humanity. There's much of what I used to admire in your father in you, Marcus. Very well. Go now, and tell the Jew that my terms are that they all come out before sunset, without their arms. No treaty with them. I propose to hang Eleazar from the cross as soon as I get him. And every third man. The rest of the men I'll blind and let go free as a token of Roman clemency. All right. Tell him that. And if we hear nothing and see nothing, then we attack at dawn. Is that understood?'

'Yes, sir. Thank you sir.'

As he turned to go, the General called after him: 'Remember, Marcus. At dawn!'

Once again, the trail from the camp was left behind him. The sun was still high overhead, barely past its hottest, roasting the valley and the soldiers who laboured under it, bringing the finishing touches to the man-made ramp that would take them storming into Masada on the morrow. A few of them turned and stared at him as he walked round the side of the mountain to the bottom of the path known as the Serpent. Wearing the same clothes as when he sneaked into the fortress, carrying the potsherd with the Jewish lettering on it that acted as a pass through the lines of the Zealots.

They had been watching for him from the top, and it was Samuel ben Ezra himself, accompanied by his silent sister, Rachel, who greeted him on the narrow, winding road to the summit.

They clasped hands, unable to stand abreast on the path, with the sheer wall at one elbow, and the drop to the valley below on the other. Marcus smiled at Rachel, and was both pleased and surprised when he received a shy smile in reply.

'Brother! What news from Rome?'

Marcus's face told its own tale, and the words were quickly spoken. Samuel shook his head. 'It was as I thought. They are too alike, Eleazar and your General. They are like two dogs who would rather die than let go of each other's throats.'

'It will be you Jews who do the dying.'

'Aye. But that is something that we are well used to, Marcus. And it's something that we have also learned to do somewhat well.'

Eleazar received the news of the terms for an unconditional surrender immediately with a face of stone, seated in style amid his council. As Marcus knew they would, they rejected it out of hand, all of them preferring to fight to the last man and to the last drop of their blood.

Yet, that was not quite the answer that Eleazar gave him to carry back. He spoke briefly, and his voice was pitched low. The chamber where they met had other rooms branching off it and Marcus was conscious of the words being repeated like a series of echoes to the rest of the people of Masada who had gathered to hear them. Nearly all of the thousand folk were there, with only a few of the men still engaged in the last dregs of the fight against the Romans.

'We hear your words, and we are grateful to you, truly grateful, for your efforts in bringing them to us. Yet we say this. To everything there is a season. And a time for every purpose under heaven. That is what our holy books tell us. They say that there is a time to live. To sow corn, and to reap the harvest. I say to you that there is a time to fight. There is also a time to die. That is all, and you may go freely back to your camp.'

The audience was over. Samuel pressed Marcus to return to

his room for a last meal and a drink of some wine that he'd been saving.

'No point in saving it any longer and letting your barbarians have it all tomorrow.'

Strangely, he seemed to have recovered all of his old spirits, and laughed as he poured out the sweet red wine. 'Should be good. Stole it myself from one of your wagon trains a few months ago.'

As they sipped it, with Rachel sitting silent in one corner of the room, Marcus pondered on the last words of Eleazar.

'Samuel?'

'What is it my brother?'

'He said that there was a time to fight. That I understand. But he also said that there was a time to die. Are they not the same?'

'In the holy book from which that comes, they are not put like that. I can't think why he said that, unless . . .'

'Unless what?'

Samuel got up and replenished his goblet, bringing more over for Marcus. He offered some to Rachel, who smiled quickly up at him, and shook her head, shyly, like a little sparrow.

'Unless he's going to do what he once talked about. He was shouted down then. Now, I wonder. Now the people may be in the mood for it.'

'For what?' shouted Marcus, his patience running out as the Jew paced the floor, seeming to commune only with himself.

'Death. Death for all of us.'

'Samuel.' Marcus was really astounded by the depth of gloom in his friend's voice. 'Of course he intends that you are all going to die. Some may be wounded and some may be taken. But there is no way out. Unless Eleazar has some of his . . . what in Hades do you call them? Some angels flying down with their wings all on fire and pluck you off the top of this damned heap of baked rock. Is that what he hopes for? Of course he means you to die.'

The young Zealot got up off the bed and came and sat closer to Marcus, looking sideways at Rachel as she sat watching them by the fireplace, idly running dead ashes through her long thin fingers. When he spoke again, his voice was as dead as the ashes.

'I am near sure of what he plans. It is not just death fighting against you. That is certain, and that would be the way of the lion. No. He plans the way of the mouse. I think that he intends that we should all kill ourselves before you even make your last attack.'

There was a sudden, deep silence, like throwing a small pebble down a dry well, and waiting for it to hit the bottom, and waiting and waiting. Marcus put down his goblet of wine, untouched, and looked at Samuel in amazement.

'He asks a warrior to slay himself? And all of his family? Without carrying the fight to the last! By Mithras! The man is mad.'

'No. You fail to understand his thinking. To a Roman, it is no great sin to kill oneself, even be it to purge some great crime. Or some incompetence. Like a General who has lost a battle through his errors. Is that not so?'

'Aye. Or for some imagined slight or disgrace.' He thought back to his father. The body, lying on its side in a welter of drying blood, the hilt of his sword sticking out from his stomach.

'Then Eleazar thinks that by doing this, we will rob you of the victory. By doing this, the name of Masada will be remembered through all the ages as the place where this happened. The Romans will be forgotten, and the Jews will remain.'

'Martyrs!' he spat contemptuously.

Samuel drained his goblet, wiping his mouth on the patched sleeve of his tunic. 'Is it better to die unmarked and forgotten?'

Marcus shook his head. 'I know not which side you stand for. Do you support Eleazar, if that be his plan, or are you against it?'

Rachel stood up, and brought over the jar of wine, but both men shook their heads. She went back to her place and sat down, keeping her eyes on their faces, as though she was trying to follow what they were saying.

'It is this way, my brother. History, if I am correct, will say that the way of Eleazar may be right. For me ... for me, I prefer life. And for my sister also. If this is what comes to pass, then I might choose to die on the wall, or making a last run for safety with Rachel. We will see.'

'Aye, brother. Perhaps we make rings in the smoke, and it may not happen. And there will be a great slaughter on the walls when the sun shows his face over the hills away there to the east.'

'Perhaps.'

Just at that moment, as though he'd been waiting for the conversation to end, a man came running along the corridor, his sandals making flat, flapping noises on the bare stones. As he went past, he called in to them: 'Samuel ben Ezra! A meeting tonight. Eleazar wishes to talk to all people in Masada. All must attend.'

Marcus and Samuel looked at each other, and neither of them spoke.

When it was discovered by the Zealots that Marcus had chosen not to go down again from the mountain, there was a deal of hostility, and it was Eleazar who saved him from more than just words. Raising that great horn of a voice, he shouldered aside the dissidents with naked blades in their hands.

'Let him stay! What harm can come? If he doesn't return this night, then the Romans will think either that we have slain him or that he still argues the case. In either case, it will make not the least difference to their plans. Come the breaking of the first light, they will be here, with their rams and their javelins. The fire and the sword will still ravage Masada if one young boy is here or no.'

It was nearly dark. The fighting of the day was over, and an odd hush had fallen over the brooding peak. The sun was setting in a pool of crimson, sinking in blood. Dark blue clouds splashed over the horizon, like clenched fists menacing the fortress.

Over to the side of the camp where the Roman ramp threatened, a fire still glowed. During the late afternoon, the Legion had used some of their thousands of prisoners of war, many of them Jewish, and brought up a great battering-ram. They'd launched an attack on the outer wall above the ramp, and broken a wide breach in it. During the assault, part of the inner defences had caught fire, and it had taken every effort from the Zealots to keep the blaze under control. Samuel had told

Marcus that he thought the Romans could have taken Masada there and then if they'd wished, but they had deliberately fallen back to wait for the grand attack on the next morning.

Dusk lay heavy over the fortress, and everywhere the men and women were making their way to the south-eastern corner of the rock, where they had their living quarters, and where Eleazar ben Ya'ir was to address them. Many of them carried torches, giving the area a strange, almost festival feeling. Somewhere, one of the men began to sing. What sounded to Marcus a tuneless dirge, it was taken up by other men, though none of the women joined in at all.

Marcus stood with Samuel and his sister. Rachel wore a long gown of black, with a hood that she pulled up over her head. Samuel had put on his best red cloak, and wore a silver-hilted sword that looked to Marcus very much as though it might once have belonged to a Roman officer, but he held his peace.

When Eleazar appeared, flanked by several Zealots of high rank, he was dressed in his finest clothes. A suit of linked silver plates, over a simple leather tunic. Bright-coloured sandals, and a heavy sword at his side. The firelight flickered off his armour, throwing red sparks among the front rows of his listeners. Samuel had whispered to Marcus that the whole of the community was there, apart from the young children and a handful of veterans who were acting as sentries. Even some of the wounded and ill were there, carried on pallets from the hospital, their bandages white and shining. Except where the blood stood out in black patches.

It was completely dark when Eleazar finally held up his hand for silence. The talk whispered away into the blackness, whirled by the wind into the void that hung around the great mountain.

'Brothers and sisters, the time has now come for us to make an ending of this conflict. I was here when Menahem took this place from the Romans. That was seven years ago. I knew the renegade Yoseph ben Matatyahu, who now calls himself Flavius Josephus. Many things have come to pass during these years. And few of them have been good. One by one our plans have died barren, and now there is only one outpost left to us. It is this great fortress of Masada.'

He was taken by a coughing fit, and when he resumed, his

voice sounded less strong, but it still carried effortlessly to the back of the crowd that stood huddled together in the light of the flickering torches.

'All is lost to us. The wall is breached, and the hill that the Romans have forced our brothers to make has finally reached our doors. On the morrow, they will come and we will not be able to deny them entrance. We were the very first to raise the banner of revolt. We are the last to carry it on. Others of our brethren have been surprised and taken, and will now live out their lives in slavery. That need not be our lot. There is another way.'

'Tell us, Eleazar! Tell us another way, and by the Living God we'll take it!' called out a tall, bearded man, whom Samuel identified in a whisper as one of the leaders of one of the most respected religious families on the rock, Shimeon ben Yoezer.

His cry was taken up by others, the noise swelling until their Commander drew his sword and held it up so that the flames danced along the blade.

'We have been given the freedom to die *in* freedom. This is something that our enemies can do nothing to hinder. They may have crushed our revolt, and burned our most holy city. They may have our dead bodies, but they shall never take our spirits. Let our wives die before they are abused by the Romans, and our children before they ever taste of the bitter fruit of slavery.'

As he spoke, so Samuel translated his words to Marcus, standing at his elbow. At this point, there were those among the women, and some among the men who were openly weeping.

'We will destroy all of our shekels, and all of our possessions, so that they find nothing here of worth for all of their endeavours. But we shall leave the food and the drink that we have as a sign that it was not a desperation at our wants that led us to this. Each man shall slay his family, and then we shall bestow the sacrament upon each other, and so shall we be preserved.'

There was a movement among the crowd, like wheat dancing before the strong wind, and Eleazar flourished his blade, his voice rising to a great crescendo.

'Brothers! Sisters! Let them that come after say that the

people of Masada were they who chose. Freely. And that they chose freedom before slavery!'

Ironically, by a strange twist of fate, Marcus was to read a report of those very words, from the man Eleazar had mentioned. The traitor Jew who called himself Flavius Josephus. But that was many years later and under the most odd circumstances.

There could be not the least doubt that the whole of the Zealots were behind their leader, and they called and shouted their approval of this macabre plan. One of their warriors even fell on his sword there and then, crying out that he would be the first to give his life for the cause.

Eleazar quietened the hysteria that had sprung up, suggesting that all should spend the evening with their families, and that they should join together in prayer at the middle of the night, and then commence their sacrifice. With that the Zealots all dispersed to their quarters.

Samuel tugged at Marcus's sleeve. 'I would talk with you, my brother. A small matter of settling a debt that lies between us.'

EIGHT

Rachel wept as she sat in the corner of their room, listening to the wailing and praying that sounded all through the old palace of Herod, in every room around them. Marcus and Samuel ignored her, as they ignored the babble of the Zealots as they prepared for their mass suicide.

'Samuel, my brother. You realize what you are doing? You go against your Commander. If you live and we are not slaughtered by your sentries, then you will walk all of your days in the knowledge that you are the man who turned his back upon Masada. Can you live with that?'

The Jew nodded slowly. 'I have thought of this, Marcus. I wish to live and to fight. Nothing more. And I see no reason for Rachel to die like a butchered calf in the shambles that this palace will become. It will serve no purpose.'

There was no way that Marcus could sway his friend, and there was no real reason why he wished to even try. In Samuel's place, he had not the least doubt that he would have done the same. Such a fatalistic acceptance of death was not in his nature, and in that also they were alike.

'So. You will go to the prayers, and I will stay here. Then, while all the men are killing their wives and their women and their children, you will come back here. The sentries will have been withdrawn, and we will hazard the path of the Serpent. It is not without danger, my brother.'

For the first time in an age, Samuel put his head back and laughed, the sound making his sister look up with a disapproving frown. She stared at Marcus, as though she would blame him for her brother's levity in the face of such a moment, then was unable to resist a smile herself when she saw the contrite expression on the face of the young Roman.

They passed the time talking quietly of things of no great moment. Samuel asked about Marcus's parents, and he told him a little of what had come to pass in Britain. In his turn, the Jew spoke of his own parents, and how they had died in a fire started in a city to the north, some said by the Romans who wished to put the blame on the Zealots. But for the most part they talked of horses they had ridden and fights they had fought. Since the girl could not understand what they spoke of, they even talked about maids that they had laid.

And both spoke a little more than was true, in the way of such young men.

At midnight, the call came for all men, and boys past the age of a certain religious significance that Marcus didn't understand, to go to the main chamber of the old palace. It was at this moment that all of the sentries were withdrawn, as the Romans would never attack at such a time. Rachel and Marcus were left alone in the room, with no common language.

She offered him some dry figs, and he took them from her hands, smiling his thanks. Rachel then brought him some water, cool from a pitcher of earthenware, and again he smiled to her to show his pleasure. And she returned his smile, and so they passed the time until the prayers were over and her brother came back again to them.

'It is done, brother. Eleazar took his leave of every man there, and each swore his trust to him. After I have stabbed my sister to the heart I must go to the next room, and there, upon the lots we drew, I have to stab my neighbour. Then my turn will come to feel the iron bite into my guts. And so on and so on until Eleazar is the last man left, and then it will be his turn to fall on his own sword.'

'Then there's not a lot of time. Come on. We must get to the path.'

Rachel still wore her dark gown, and Marcus his tunic. Samuel reversed his red cloak, so that it showed near black in the pale moonlight. Like ghosts through a graveyard. A graveyard in which not all of the bodies were yet dead. The small houses they left behind were mostly showing pale yellow lamps. And from them came the cries of mothers as their children were killed by their husbands. Who then turned the blades on their wives.

The wind had dropped again, and the dust lay still between the ravaged buildings of the fortress. The moon hung, like a pale silver sickle, casting grey shadows across the courts and passages. The path to the Serpent road down the mountain would normally have bristled with armed guards, but it now stood deserted.

Rachel walked close to her brother, and she stopped with a start when they heard a piercing scream come from one of the houses. Samuel looked back, as though he was trying to locate exactly where it had come from.

'That sounds like the voice of Sarah. There was a time when she and I . . . well, that was an eternity ago. There will be some who will not leap winking to their deaths, despite the words of Eleazar ben Ya'ir. Maybe your soldiers will not find a place of silent death when they come here on the morrow.'

Before they realized it, they were past where the last of the guard-posts would have stood, poised at the top of the treacherous winding path to the valley below. From where they stood, they could actually see the lights of the vast Roman camp a thousand feet below them.

'We will be down there in a little over the hour, my brother,' whispered Samuel, taking the arm of his sister.

'Dog!'

The word was hissed at them by a giant figure that leaped up from out of the earth, a sword slicing at them in an arc of death. All three leaped back, Samuel pushing the girl clear behind them. Both men drawing their weapons. The Jew his sword, and the Roman his short-bladed dagger.

The man blocked the path, and the only way down was past him. There was no alternative.

'So. Eleazar was right. He said that there would be those who would value their lives more than the cause, and who would worm their way out on their bellies. Go back, Samuel ben Ezra, and play the part of a man, though you act now like a shivering woman.'

'Benjamin. I would not kill you, but I must go.'

'And your friend, the Roman spy. You may return to your quarters, ben Ezra, and your sister. But the Roman will stay and die here.'

Because of the narrowness of the path, it was impossible for the two men to come at the sentry together. Marcus thought for a moment of the chances of throwing his knife and killing the

Jew, but the light was poor, and the distance uncertain. And the man wore armour.

'I will not wait for you, Samuel. If you turn not and go back, then I will call out for aid. There are others about the wall that will come to my aid. Now!'

Samuel was slightly in front of Marcus, and the Roman was partly shielded by his body. Cautiously, he slipped his hand through the belt at the back, clenching his fist, keeping the knife ready in his other hand.

'Trust me,' he whispered in Samuel's ear.

'What's that?' barked the guard.

Without another word, Marcus pushed his friend forward as hard as he could. Straight at the sentry. So constricted was the space, that it was the one form of attack that the man had not expected, as to leap forward in that way would put both lives at hazard. Benjamin cried out in alarm, and tried to get his sword up to parry the charge, but he was too late, and the blade was only half-raised when they hit him. The force of the impact sent him staggering back, feet scrabbling for a hold on the furthest edge of the mighty drop, letting go of his sword, throwing his arms round Samuel to prevent himself plunging over the brink.

Behind them, Marcus heard Rachel cry out in shock, as the three of them posed like some tableau, frozen on the edge of eternity. The guard gasped, head thrown back, his beard jutting towards the stars, tipping over the void. Samuel kept still, prevented from falling by Marcus's hand clasping his belt. In a moment, Benjamin would recover his nerve and realize that as long as the Roman held Samuel, and he also held him, then they were all safe. Once he realized that, then he would call out for aid.

If he had done that, then Marcus was resolved to let his friend go, whatever the loss, and try to make for safety with the girl. Up on the great rock, he would be at an impossible disadvantage against the Zealots who would know every inch of it.

Bracing himself back, Marcus looked down, seeing where the sentry's fingers were locked whitely around Samuel. The guard was making soft mewing sounds, deep in his throat, still terrified at the prospect of the plummeting death. Knife hilt firm in his right hand, the young Roman hacked suddenly at the Jew's fingers, feeling blood spurt over his wrist and arm.

'Please.' The word was in Latin. Quiet. Like a child pleading for an extra sweetmeat before being sent to bed.

Marcus sawed away, feeling the blade grate on the finger bones, forcing the hands loose, then reaching over Samuel's shoulder and lunging with the dripping dagger at the guard's face, catching him in the mouth. There was the sickening sound of breaking teeth, splintering under the thrust. The knife sliced open the side of the man's mouth, giving him the odd appearance in the pale moonlight of a lopsided grin. The point skewered his tongue, pinning it to the roof of his mouth, making it impossible for him to cry out.

Blood poured over the sentry's chest and neck, flowing in a torrent down his throat making him choke. His mutilated hands finally let go of Samuel, reaching up to try and force away the dagger. But in so doing, he lost his grip on life, and slowly, very slowly, toppled backwards, sandals scratching at the edge of the rocky path, arms thrown up, and eyes staring helplessly at the men who had killed him.

The hilt of the knife was pulled from Marcus's hands, made slippery with the blood, and remained in Benjamin's mouth, like a monstrous fish-hook, the silver glittering as he fell away. With his other hand, the Roman pulled Samuel back to safety, while they listened for the noise of the body falling.

Perhaps the wind took it away, but they listened in vain. The body had gone as silently as though the Furies had plucked him from the empty air.

'That was too close, my brother,' said Samuel, panting with the shock and the struggle.

Rachel came running and embraced him, looking at Marcus as though she wished to say something, then thinking better of it and burying her face in her brother's chest, recoiling when she found her cheeks slobbered with the warm blood of the dead guard.

'Samuel. We had best be gone from here. If there is one guard, then it is safer to guess that there might be others. The path will be perilous at night, and the lines of my people are not far. It would not be well to die at the hands of a Roman soldier after escaping from a Zealot's sword.'

Together, helping the girl, they made their way down the perilous Serpent path, leaving the great brown bulk of the mountain rising behind and above them. The sounds from Masada seemed to have died away, and the only noise was the wind, blowing around the hill, whipping up the sand and dust and driving it into their eyes.

Samuel led the way, familiar with the twists and turns of the sinuous path, followed by Rachel, with Marcus bringing up the rear. They were, he guessed, something over halfway down when they heard a challenge from one of the Roman soldiers who guarded the path from any escaping Zealots.

'Stand there! Who comes? Identify yourself!'

'Marcus Julius Britannicus, auxiliary scout, attached to the staff of General Flavius Silva and the Tenth Legion, with two Jewish prisoners.'

Warily, the looming figure of a tall Centurion came towards them out of the darkness. 'Is that you, Marcus? We thought the Jews must have served you up in a stew by now. Is all well?'

'Aye, Antonius. All well. I think that the attack will go well on the morrow. Now, I must pass with these prisoners.'

They filed past, Marcus noting that there were at least half a hundred men scattered along the lower slopes, all armed and armoured. Ready for the morning. At the same time as the main force was to attack the ramp, there would also be smaller diversionary forces striking up the two paths.

'All that will be for naught, when dawn comes,' commented Marcus once they were past.

'Aye. True enough, brother. Why did you not tell the officer of that?'

'I have a reason, brother. I wanted only to get past without him insisting on sending an escort, and there is another reason. One for myself alone.'

Only a few minutes later they were again on the level ground of the plain below. The camp was in a state of turmoil, with men and horses in a whirl of movement. Trumpets were blowing, and lines of torches flared across the valley. The side of the rock that they were on was comparatively free of soldiers, the great bulk of the Legion concentrating on the ramp to the west. Away to the one side, there was a free way from the area, leading to a road along the coast.

Marcus stopped. 'There lies your way, Samuel ben Ezra. My brother. I can take you no further. Now you stand on your own and you must go with haste. There are still some hours to sunrise. Now go.'

The Jew stood and looked at him, his eyes serious. The moon was sinking slowly away, but there was a deal of light still sprinkled out from the pool at the camp. Rachel waited behind her brother, shrouded in her cloak, only the deep pits of her eyes glittering.

'I thank you for seeing us to safety, my brother. That is another debt paid in full. Now nothing lies between us. I tell you; I have had enough of debts.'

'And I. There shall be no more between you and me. All is paid. I think it will be well our paths do not cross again.'

The young Zealot shook his head. 'Perhaps. Yet I feel in my bones that we shall look upon each other again before we both take the trip from which no man returns. Perhaps. Come, let us not part though on this gloomy note. I thank you, my Roman brother. The enemy who is my friend. It has been an honour to know you, Marcus Julius Britannicus.'

'And I to know you, Samuel ben Ezra. Now, time runs away from us, like sand through a glass. Go. And may your Gods go with you.'

They clasped hands formally, then embraced, laying their heads on each other's shoulders, and hugging for a moment. Then pulling apart, and looking at each other. Rachel tugged at her brother's cloak, and whispered something to him. He smiled at Marcus.

'My sister would embrace you as her brother, and as a token of her thanks.'

'There is no need. Tell her that it has been my honour to know her.'

Samuel spoke quickly, but she again said something to him, obviously pressing him.

'Still she insists that she bids you farewell.'

'Then I accept her embrace.'

Her face downcast, Rachel stepped lightly nearer to him, then put her cheek up for him to kiss. Deep within the shadow of her hood, she was invisible to her brother, who was, in any case gazing over the plain, trying to see if there were any Roman patrols out.

As Marcus dutifully kissed her softly on the face, she suddenly brought up her arms and threw them round his neck, forcing her lips against his mouth. Taken by surprise, he hardly responded at all, until her tongue poked at his lips, forcing its way in, and roaming about, caressing and sucking at his tongue. It was more the kiss of a wanton lover, than the chaste thanks that he'd expected, but he held her close, and kissed her, his eyes watching the turned back of Samuel, not knowing how he would respond if he saw what was happening within the hood of her gown.

Finally, panting, her body trembling, the young girl pulled away, and whispered something to him. Something that he didn't understand, but that he guessed could only mean one thing. And that fact of her love troubled him, and lay with him for many years after.

Samuel turned round, and Marcus didn't know what he'd seen and what he'd guessed, but he said nothing, merely holding out his hand for his sister to take. Slowly, looking back over his shoulder, the young Jew set off away from the rock of Masada, that still hung its giant shadow across all of the land. When they were so far away that they could scarcely see each other, Samuel drew his sword and waved it high in the still air, so that the setting moon glinted on it. Marcus waved his hand in return.

Then, they were gone.

The Centurion Antonius was surprised to see Marcus coming back again, wanting to go up to the fortress once more.

'It lacks only two hours to dawn. And then we shall attack. Why not wait and make the climb with us?'

'No. There is one thing that I must do there. Fear not. The Zealots will not harm me, knowing the final assault is so close. And none of our soldiers are likely to mistake me for one of those bearded Jews, are they? But, I would ask one favour. Can I borrow a sword from someone? I left my dagger in the throat of one of their sentries somewhere up there and I fear I cannot ask him for it.'

With a short laugh, the officer found a weapon for him. The simple, functional stabbing sword of the common foot-soldier, and he buckled it on. Antonius made a last attempt to dissuade him from going, but Marcus was determined, and they finally let him through.

'I hope the bitch's worth it!' called the Centurion as he vanished round one of the many bends in the path.

The moon was gone by the time he neared the top of Masada and the whole place was shrouded in pitch darkness. Although he took the greatest care, the path was quite unguarded, and he was able to step out on the great flat expanse of the fortress unchallenged.

It was silent. Not the silence of a sleeping town, but the total silence of a tomb. Nothing moved. The smell of smoke caught at his throat, and he coughed. None of the Jews' livestock made a sound, and he guessed that the mass suicide had now been carried through. Before he stepped down over the surrounding wall he looked over to the east, and saw the first pale hint of the coming dawn. Time was running out fast. Over on the side of the mighty ramp, he could hear the hustle and bustle as the army prepared for the attack. Officers shouted, and he heard the crack of whips on flesh as some stubborn slave was slow in obeying an order.

Marcus walked slowly through the burning palace, awed by the desolation he saw. His sword was in his hand, but there was no need for it. Every room he went in had its quota of the dead. Wives, children, babies, men. All lay quietly where they had fallen, their faces at peace. Most had died with blows through the neck. The blood was drying on many of the corpses, and there were already flies gorging themselves on the feast.

Close to the Water Gate, near the northern edge of the fortress, stood a large cluster of buildings, all blazing fiercely, the crackling of the dry wood sounding unnaturally loud amidst the quiet. Sparks were thrown high in the night air, glowing red dots that spun upwards until they vanished. He guessed that the sight of the fires must have worried the officers on the ramp, but that Flavius Silva was suspecting a last trick by the Zealots and was waiting for first light.

The three tiers of the northern palace dropped away from him, with its ornate columns and wall paintings that Samuel had talked of. It was there that the leaders of the rebellion had lived, and it was there that he thought to find the body of Eleazar. Stepping carefully among the rubble and wreckage that had been left, pushing aside a charred beam that had fallen across the passage, Marcus made his way towards the tip of the mountain.

The wood clattered as it fell, and suddenly he heard a sound he had not thought to hear on Masada. The voice of a man, crying out in the tongue of the Jews.

Sword probing the air in front of him, Marcus stepped through the ruined apartments. Climbing down lower and lower, across the middle terrace, into the bottom level, with its fine decorations. The fire seemed to be growing in violence and it was obvious that the Zealots had carried out their threat to leave nothing for the Romans to claim as victory.

The voice came again, much nearer. The voice of a man in great pain and distress. Coming from the small bath-house that stood open to his right. Untouched by the fire, it was a square building, hanging in space over the edge of Masada. He went in, and saw two bodies. A young child, and a woman, about twenty, both with their throats slit, the woman with a long plait of hair dabbled with the lake of blood where she and the baby lay.

And in one corner, squat and hunched up like a toad, was the Commander of the fortress, Eleazar ben Ya'ir. When he saw the young man, with sword in hand, his face changed from one of pain to one of shock, and he spoke in his halting Latin.

'So. It is dawn?'

He wore the armour of silver that he'd been wearing before, but it was heavily stained with blood all down the right side, around where the shoulder wound had been. And his leg lay crook'd under him. As far as Marcus could see, he was weaponless.

'No. I came back. To see what the manner of your dying would be. Yet you live. Within the hour there will be soldiers all over this place, and yet you live. Why?'

'This damned cut. It burst open as I threw one of the torches. I had slain my family, and I intended to come back here and lie with them. But the loss of blood weakened me, and I fell on those steps. My sword slid like a stone across a frozen pool and now rests a thousand feet below.'

Marcus wearily leaned his hand on the cool stone of the wall and looked down at the man. 'You cannot bleed to death, and you cannot crawl to throw yourself after your sword.' He laughed. 'After all those fine words. The only man the Legion will find here is you. The Commander of the Zealots. It will make up to Flavius Silva for what you've done to dash the cup of victory from his lips.'

'You're a young man, Roman. You have much of life left to you. As you come to the end of it, whenever that may be, then think back to the moment you denied a man the chance of dying as he wished. If you leave me, they will carry me down, and patch me up. Then scourge me, and bear me to a cross of wood and hammer nails through the palms of my hands and through my ankles. Eventually, mad with thirst and pain, I shall die with my lungs choked.'

Smiling, Marcus leaned down by him. 'And you will have deserved it, many times over for the deaths that you carry on your shoulders. I shall shed no tears for you, Eleazar.'

And he turned from the scene of death to walk in the cool air of the coming dawn. The wind was carrying the smoke away from the northern end of the palace, and there it was fresh and clean. He was about to shut the door, when the voice stopped him.

'Samuel told me of you. Of your father being high-born, and a noble. Would he have left an enemy to die thus?'

It was a simple question, asked with no heat or anger or self-pity. Rather in a mild, curious manner, like a teacher seeking an answer to a problem of logic. Yet it hit home better than anything could have done.

His hand on the door-latch, Marcus stopped. His fingers toyed with the stone round his neck, and he looked up at the sky. It was already getting lighter, and in a few minutes the Romans would be all over Masada. Slowly, he took the short sword in his hand, feeling the point against his thumb.

And tossed it in the room.

There were words of thanks, but he didn't bother to wait and hear them. He swiftly left the lower terrace and went back up the steep stairs, ready to greet his comrades as they came over the top of the ramp, and walked among the silent ruins of the great hill of the dead.

They saw nothing but a perfect solitude within the place, and a terrible fire. At length they gave a great cry as it had been a battering-ram, to try if any came out. They quickly cut their way through the fire to the palace, and there came upon the multitude of the slain but they took no pleasure in it, though it had been done to their enemies. Nor could they do other than wonder at the great courage and at the immovable contempt for death which so great a number had shown, when they carried through such an act as that was.

From the 'Works Of Flavius Josephus',
37–100(?) A.D.

NINE

'Come brother. Strike. I have had enough of debts.'

In the broiling sun of the Colosseum of Rome, Marcus the gladiator, called 'Vulpus', stood still and looked at the face of the man in front of him. The Jew that he had crippled, and who now waited the final blow. Samuel ben Ezra. Some eight years older than that night on Masada, but still the same man.

In all the tiers, soaring up into the blue sky, the mob were on their feet, screaming for the death of the Jew. The editor again jabbed down his thumb, his face showing worry at the delay. The moment was passing, and the crowd were fickle.

The chant of 'Death! Death!! Death!!!' grew louder, drowning out everything else. Marcus held his sword loose at his side, unable to think. Stunned by the appearance of this ghost from the long-dead past.

Ben Ezra spoke again, his voice more urgent. 'Strike, brother. I am the enemy you must kill, my friend.'

Poppaea was on her feet with the rest, almost fainting with the swell of sexual pleasure. It wasn't like Vulpus to keep them all waiting. Maybe this one was going to be really special. Her thighs were hot and moist, and she bit her fingers until blood flowed from the quick of the nail.

'Death!!!!'

Marcus stepped in closer, and stared deep into the eyes of his friend.

'Farewell, brother,' he said, raising his sword.

While the crowd cheered and cheered.